MW01410001

Geronimo's Kids

NUMBER SIXTEEN:
*Elma Dill Russell Spencer Series
in the West and Southwest*

Geronimo's Kids

A Teacher's Lessons on the Apache Reservation

Rev. Robert S. Ove and H. Henrietta Stockel

Texas A&M University Press
College Station

Copyright © 1997 by Rev. Robert S. Ove and H. Henrietta Stockel
Manufactured in the United States of America
All rights reserved
First edition
04 03 02 01 00 99 98 97   5 4 3 2 1

The paper used in this book meets the minimum requirements
of the American National Standard for Permanence
of Paper for Printed Library Materials, Z39.48-1984.
Binding materials have been chosen for durability.

∞

Library of Congress Cataloging-in-Publication Data

Ove, Robert S.
    Geronimo's kids : a teacher's lessons on the Apache reservation / Robert S. Ove and H. Henrietta Stockel. — 1st ed.
       p.   cm. — (Elma Dill Russell Spencer series in the West and Southwest ; no. 16)
    Includes bibliographical references.
    ISBN 0-89096-774-1
    1. Chiricahua Indians—New Mexico—Whitetail—Social life and customs. 2. Ove, Robert S. 3. Teachers—New Mexico—Mescalero Indian Reservation—Biography. 4. Whitetail (N.M.) 5. Mescalero Indian Reservation (N.M.) I. Stockel, H. Henrietta, 1938–   .
II. Title. III. Series.
E99.C68093   1997
978.9'65—dc21   97-18561
                                                                          CIP

Contents

List of Illustrations	vii
Preface	ix
Acknowledgments	xxi
Introduction	xxv

CHAPTERS

1. Remembering Whitetail — 3
2. The Whitetail Day School — 22
3. If Only I Had Known . . . — 36
4. The Old Timers at Whitetail — 46
5. Religion, Other White Folks, and Chiricahua Apache Justice — 85
6. Talks with the Kids and the Cook — 104
7. Leaving Whitetail — 125

Notes	135
Bibliography	143
Index	145

Illustrations

following page 84

Geronimo
Original Bureau of Indian Affairs
    hand carved sign
Teacherage at Whitetail
Chiricahua girls
Whitetail class, 1948–49
Robert Geronimo
Levi Hostosevit
Charles Istee
Leroy Coonie
Myrtis Kanseah
Jasper Kanseah, Jr.
Delores Enjady
Eugene Chihuahua and family
Vernon D. Simmons
Dorcie and Isaac Kazhe and family
Melvin Kanseah
Berle Kanseah
Ulysses Jolsanny
Wynelle Enjady
Tribal store
Dutch Reformed Church
Charley Smith
Ouida Geronimo Miller
Modeling ceremonial puberty dresses

Preface

When Robert S. Ove arrived at Whitetail on the Mescalero Apache Reservation in 1948 to begin teaching, many of the older Chiricahua Apaches he found there—the parents and grandparents of the children he was to teach—were the survivors of nearly thirty years of incarceration by the U.S. government. The new teacher had heard of Geronimo and his warrior band, of course—who had not?—and was vaguely familiar with their deeds, but he never really, consciously, linked his new job to those folks. To Ove, what mattered was that he had landed a teaching position when no one else would hire him, and, as part of the arrangement with the Bureau of Indian Affairs, had taken a bride.

Then in his very early twenties, Bob Ove was a tall, self-conscious, awkward, timid young man on his first job. Although initially anxious about his ability to do his job and about living on the reservation, he was delighted to be employed in an idyllic setting high in the mountains of south-central New Mexico. To sweeten the pot, he and his wife were permitted to live in a furnished house provided by the Bureau of Indian Affairs for only twenty-five dollars per month. And so, there he was, as if fallen from the sky, an innocent, naive young white man amid members of one of the fiercest groups of American Indians ever to resist the westward expansion of the United States of America.

If even a few of the frightening myths about the Chiricahua Apaches had been true, Ove would have had reason to fear them. But these people, like Native Americans elsewhere across the country, were not at all as the media depicted them. In the middle to late 1800s the tragic events that had occurred in the Southwest had been emblazoned on the public consciousness. Contemporary newspaper headlines kept the focus on the West, screaming out of Arizona and New Mexico to let the nation know in huge, boldface letters that the Chiricahua Apaches were savages: cold-blooded murderers, bloodthirsty killers who enjoyed torturing their captives. That was one side of it.

From the Apaches' point of view, however, they were only protecting what their one god, *Ussen,* had given them—a homeland that met their basic needs for food, shelter, medicine, and, perhaps most important, water. In the desert of the Southwest, water was a precious commodity, something to be cherished, protected, and defended to the death, if necessary. When thousands of easterners moved into Apache country, fencing the land, grazing livestock, mining, and competing for valuable natural resources such as water, the Chiricahuas understood that their homeland was being invaded. Resistance was their first reaction, and Geronimo's people certainly resisted, with a might and force that astonished the United States government and its military arm.

The Indians eventually lost, but it took nearly one quarter of the entire United States Army to find and convince the last Apache holdouts, thirty-five Chiricahua men, women, and children, to surrender in 1886. Then, and only then, did they give up, and only because Geronimo feared that if they kept fighting, the entire Apache people would be destroyed. He had General George Crook's word on that. "You must make up your own mind whether you will stay out on the warpath or surrender unconditionally. If you stay out," warned Crook during the surrender negotiations, "I'll keep after you and kill the last one, if it takes fifty years."[1]

Decades of incarceration of all the Chiricahuas—peaceful and otherwise—followed, first in Florida, then in Alabama, and finally in Oklahoma. During these years the enemy changed. No longer the government and military of the United States, the foe was now contagious diseases, unseen forces that the Apaches could not resist and had no way of stopping. Since the first contacts with Europeans, Native American peoples had been decimated by diseases to which they had no inborn resistance, but the virulence of such diseases, even some as relatively innocuous to people of European ancestry as measles, was exacerbated by poor nutrition and the unavoidability of close contact between infected and healthy individuals in the prison's close quarters. In pure numbers, more than half of the entire group of approximately 535 confined Chiricahuas perished miserably in the hot and humid prison camps, not nobly in battle as many of their ancestors had, but from the bloody coughs of tuberculosis or the high fevers of measles or the exhausting sweats of malaria. Even the children who were taken from their parents and sent away to school in Carlisle, Pennsylvania, sickened. When enough of them had died to embarrass the school's superintendent, he sent the terminally ill children back by train to their incarcerated parents.[2]

In 1913 the survivors, who numbered fewer than three hundred, were finally released after years of political rhetoric, manipulation, and machinations in Washington, D.C., and the Southwest. Some of the newly freed Chiricahuas decided to remain in Oklahoma, and they received land allotments in established communities not far from their last prison site, Fort Sill. A larger number, those whose lives became entwined with Bob Ove's, settled on the Mescalero Apache Reservation in New Mexico.[3]

Before the Chiricahuas arrived, the area known as Whitetail, to be their home, was populated only by wild game. Soon, amidst the high grasses and tall evergreens, government housing popped up in the form of uninsulated two- or four-room log cabins with porches. In most cases, furnishings provided by the government were in sad condition—torn couches, battered tables, and wobbly chairs. Only a few refinements were apparent: women hung tattered curtains in some windows, and rugs in a few homes kept feet off bare boards.

Fueled by wood from the surrounding forest, potbelly stoves provided heat; a few homes had propane. Most houses had an indoor sink in the kitchen. When pipes froze, people had to come to the school to draw water from the outside tap and haul it back home in buckets and cans.

Kitchens contained only the most rudimentary cooking equipment. Perhaps reflecting traditional practices, sometimes the Apaches would cook outdoors around an open fire and would eat on dishes that resembled tin pie plates. Empty jelly jars and old tin cans often served as dishes. A few elders ate with hunting knives wiped clean on pants or sleeves, as they had done in days long gone. Glasses and cups, barely enough for the family and a guest or two, looked as though they had been accumulated from church sales over the years.

Toilet facilities usually consisted of an outhouse in the backyard. Taking a bath required heating water on the stove and pouring it into a large metal tub. To conserve precious water and fuel, bathing was often a family affair, with children using the same water one after another until everyone was clean. "We had to carry water from the creek and carry the wood from up in the mountains on our back," said Elbys Hugar, the great-granddaughter of Cochise, remembering her young years at Whitetail. "We used [the water] to cook and keep warm. We had to heat the water up outside by a fire to do our laundry and to take baths. But even though it was very hard to get by, we all were happy. We had a happy family."

From today's perspective one wonders how in the world a people could be so poor and yet happy. "Because you feel more love," Elbys Hugar said. "We can feel it within each other—the warmth of what love really is when you are poor. Hardship keeps the family close together because all of us are in need and the only thing we have for each other is love. You can show your love more when you are poor, when you're really in need. You're always willing to help others. When our relatives came on a weekend to visit us, we brought the food out, what we had, and we ate with them."[4]

No one hunted for food with bows and arrows anymore when Ove was at Whitetail, although these were still made to sell to tourists or, in the case of some of the older members of the group, just to keep the tradition alive. One of the traditional crafts Ove saw practiced at Whitetail was cradleboard (*tsach*) making. Apache mothers have always transported their young children in cradleboards, although the actual construction of the carrier has been modified. Grandmothers and mothers still sewed the traditional beaded buckskin dresses with tin can jingles for their daughters to wear during the puberty ceremonies, and the men still made the traditional Apache drums and rattles.

For income, the people began to run cows, as they had successfully done at Fort Sill. To sustain themselves they dug wells and cisterns, laid pipes, and planted and irrigated crops. Electricity arrived just before Ove's first year at Whitetail, thanks to rural electrification. Before that, candles and coal lamps provided light at night. Telephones appeared. The sound of car engines replaced the clop-clop of horses' hooves. A school was built by the government, and a church was built by the Dutch Reformed missionaries who accompanied the Chiricahuas from Fort Sill, with help from those Chiricahuas who had become Protestants. Being a resilient lot, the Chiricahuas made the best of their circumstances, and the Whitetail community began to flourish.

The Apaches mingled with people—teachers, cowboys, and others whose trade or profession brought them to Whitetail—who could teach them or help them survive in the white man's world. Like Ove, many who interacted with the Apaches were impressed by their considerable physical skills, their intelligence, their compassion, and their love for children. The kids themselves were like children everywhere—mischievous, ornery, sometimes shy, sometimes assertive, teasers, flirts, determined to defy authority. They talked to outsiders in the Apache language and howled with glee when the strangers did not understand; they got into fights, hated bathing, played with their dogs and horses, made dolls and doll clothes, lost their baby teeth, ate scoops of snow dropped into cups and flavored with syrup, picked flowers, planted seeds, and carved small bows and arrows. Most of the Apache kids played catch. Sometimes they set up teams for baseball, and sometimes they imitated the sacred *Gah'e* (traditional dancers) or pretended they were wild animals. Never did the children allow their teacher or any other non-Indian to see them playing Apache games, probably because of adult admonitions. Protecting cultural customs had become a way of life for many, particularly for those who had been prisoners of war. Even the children's traditional games were understandably treasured by those whose trust of white people had been destroyed, and it is not unreasonable to assume that the kids were told not to play this or that in front of the new teacher.

For adults at Whitetail, cards were the greatest source of entertainment during long days and nights, and gambling was almost certainly part of the action. When they were a free people, and throughout their years of imprisonment, the Chiricahuas wagered whenever they could for whatever they could—shells, stones, clothing, money, anything. Games of chance had always been popular, back as far as many could remember. In more modern times, Elbys Hugar recalled one of the older Chiricahua women, Siki, by saying, "I used to see Siki and her husband Toklanni when I went with my parents down the road. On the side of the hill they played cards, *kunkan* mostly. They used to play cards out in the open. Some people play there today, and once in a while I take part. It's a very enjoyable game. We go to Juarez, Mexico, and buy the cards. You play with two decks at a time."[5]

At Whitetail, a typical day in the life of an Apache began early. The kids had to be fed and dressed for school, and the livestock had to be tended. Women spent their days preparing meals, doing laundry, and canning food, always keeping a watchful eye on the younger children and grandchildren. When there was time for socializing, gossiping with relatives and friends was a regular pursuit. The more vigorous women occasionally walked down the mountain into town and back, a distance of nearly thirty miles each way.

The men who worked at the cow camp could be gone for up to a week or more, toiling for long hours and low pay. A few were employed in activities associated with logging and mining. Some men worked as police or fire marshals or in the tribal offices. Some hunted wild turkey and deer. Occasionally they slaughtered a cow for their own use, selling off a portion of the beef to others. The men at Whitetail did their own car repairs, which tended to be primitive. One old Nash had bailing wire wrapped the wrong way around a broken drive shaft. This vehicle, when "fixed," drove backward, causing great gales of laughter throughout the village. The car's owner enjoyed being the center of attention for a while but eventually abandoned his vehicle and used the bailing wire for other purposes; supplies at Whitetail were always short, and there had to be multiple uses for everything. Always a pragmatic people, Apaches were also thrifty about their cars. When a tire became worn, the car's owner simply fitted another old tire over the original.

To an outsider, Apaches seemed to do everything at a slow pace. Filling a tank with gas at the school's pump could take half an hour with time out for talk and a drink of water. Walking never looked hurried, nor did driving. Even talk was slow and deliberate, a reflection of traditional way of expression. The only ones who seemed to be in a rush were kids, dogs, and horses. The day revolved around meeting the immediate needs of the extended family for food, clothing, and shelter. The tempo picked up a bit during ceremonies, piñon-picking season in autumn, roundup, rodeo, harvest, and cattle and crop sales. Then spirits lifted, folks became more animated, and the air filled with a measure of excitement. But the only place at Whitetail that really ran by the clock was the school, and there even Bob Ove grew more relaxed as time passed.

The Chiricahuas' relationship with the well-intentioned instructor gradually warmed. They cautiously accepted him into their community, and some eventually shared with him a little of their history and culture. Despite their understandable wariness toward all non-Indians, they bore him no personal animosity. Robert Ove gained their trust, possibly because of his sincerity but more likely because of his profession. The Apaches have always respected education, formal or informal, and those who taught. In time he was included in some of their social activities; he became a trusted advisor to several families and attended their ceremonies. It was obvious to the Apaches that Ove took very seriously his responsibility for their children's education, and they appreciated his efforts. A few Chiricahuas allowed him to take their pictures as they went about their daily lives. He snapped Robert Geronimo, son of the great warrior, sitting on the front porch of the teacherage, relaxing and passing the time of day. There is a shot or two in his collection of Charles Istee, the only surviving son of Chief Victorio of the Warm Springs Apache band, wearing a very old slouched hat and driving a tractor on his parcel of land. Charley Smith, a powerful but humble medicine man, posed for a picture, but not wearing his traditional medicine garb. Dorcie Kazhe, the school's cook, and her children, Lynette and Peter, were the subjects of many photos. Lynette became the wife of Berle Kanseah, Ove's brightest student. Berle Kanseah is now a member of the Mescalero Apache Tribal Council and is a respected spokesman for the contemporary Chiricahuas living on the reservation.

Unfortunately, the opportunity for one very special photo never arrived. The Apache woman warrior Dahteste (known by all as "Old Lady Coonie") was still alive then. In her girlhood Dahteste had ridden with Cochise; later she had been one of two women sent by Geronimo to initiate peace talks with the U.S. Army. Although she was probably nearing one hundred years old when Ove was at Whitetail, she was still active. She participated in community life, told stories about the old days to younger Chiricahuas, and resolutely refused to speak English. Several Apaches told Ove she would kill him if he even tried to photograph her. He resisted the impulse. He has a clear recollection of her, the house she lived in with her niece, Eliza Coonie, the many stray dogs she fed, the burro that she rode up and down the road that ran through Whitetail, and Eliza's pickup truck, which Dahteste considered a family asset and moneymaker.

In the summer of 1992 when Bob Ove returned to the Mescalero Apache Reservation and Whitetail, he went straight to the collapsing walls of Dahteste's house and took pictures from every angle, much as a fashion photographer would photograph a beautiful woman. Beckoning to him was a metal trough full of discarded items that had been left near the front of her home more than forty years earlier. Stooping, he scooped out a rusty lunch pail, asked his wife to hold it up to the light, and photographed it. In the field adjacent to the Coonie house, the frame of Eliza's pickup truck lay half-buried in the ground. The former teacher tromped across the grass, turned his back to the sun, and took several shots of the truck just as a garden snake disturbed from its slumber dropped to the ground near the right fender and wiggled away. Watching Ove, I could almost hear Old Lady Coonie cackling from afar about the antics of the white man, still taking pictures at Whitetail after all these years.

Dahteste never left Whitetail. She was laid to rest somewhere in the church cemetery. Most of that forlorn burial site is overgrown now; many markers are missing, and there is no map that shows whose bones rest where. The grounds have not been tended since the last Chiricahua resident abandoned the community in the mid-1950s. By then the lure of "progress" was too appealing to ignore. Moving closer to the center of the reservation gave people easier access to the nearby towns and to U.S. Highway 70, the main route into and out of the area.

When Ove's term at Whitetail ended in 1950, the people and the place were still intact. He was not rehired, so off he went, taking with him two years' worth of experiences few non-Indians would ever know. Stashed in his baggage were dozens of slides, negatives, and prints depicting his life among the Chiricahua Apaches.

Doris Gils Ove, Bob's wife, was present during his two years at Whitetail, but she does not figure largely in this book. She did not have her husband's established role in the community, and she chose to remain in the background. The new Mrs. Ove had entered Carthage College, a Lutheran educational institution, in the fall of 1946. She and Bob became engaged shortly after they met, and the couple continued attending college for the next two years. Because Bob had to be married in order to take the job at Whitetail, Doris accepted his proposal and left Carthage without finishing her own degree. Instead, she packed up her life and moved to the reservation with her bridegroom. A city girl, an excellent pianist, a product of a cultured and refined Chicago family, she could hardly have been prepared for the kind of existence she suddenly faced. The pain of adjustment was at first eased by the scenic beauty, the clean fresh air, and the hard work necessary to make the cottage livable. Then reality set in.

Her closest friends were the school cooks, first Delores Enjady and then Dorcie Kazhe. She liked Dorcie's young children and often gave them rides on Marmaduke, the horse, or pushed them in the swing. Because initially she did not drive, she was more or less housebound during the day while Bob was teaching. When parents visited the teacherage in the evenings or on weekends to discuss their children, she frequently excused herself and walked away from the conversation. Ove tried to include her, but she seemed to prefer not to become involved.

The young couple's closest friends were other non-Indians who interacted with the Chiricahuas: Father Marcian, from the Saint Joseph's Catholic mission at Mescalero, the Leland Carls, teachers at the Mescalero school, the TeBeasts, from the Dutch Reformed Church's mission, and other mission personnel. Miles McCoy and his wife, who managed the five-and-ten-cent store in Ruidoso, occasionally made the trip to Whitetail. "Cookie," from the town drugstore, was also a rare visitor, and Bob and Doris regularly stopped at both places during their infrequent trips to Ruidoso. The isolation of Whitetail precluded most socializing. Even after Doris Ove learned to drive, there was seldom occasion for visiting outside the community.

Social events at Whitetail were limited. There were weekly dances and movies at the schoolhouse, but Mrs. Ove chose not to participate regularly in them or in the few activities scheduled at the Dutch Reformed mission at Whitetail. She polished her housekeeping skills and became an exceptional cook. In spite of her isolation, she did not seem bored or lonely or unhappy. In fact, she often sang around the house.

Robert Ove's first aim in life had been to study drama and become an actor and director. He had methodically stepped toward that goal by acting in high school plays and by starring in the senior class play. At Carthage College he majored in English and minored in psychology and music. Eventually, after he became engaged to Doris, he realized that he needed a more reliable profession, and he switched his minor to education. He qualified for a secondary school credential and did his practice teaching at a local high school. And there you have it. Except for one other item: this good fellow is now a retired Lutheran minister.

Bob Ove has always been fascinated by religious philosophy, but not by "church," which in his youth he had found dull and boring. He does admit that the Bible held his interest for a while—until halfway through Exodus when the plot fell apart.

About ten years after leaving Whitetail, Bob was once again "fooling around" with a camera, this time with one that took motion pictures. He was offered an opportunity to make "skin flicks." After he adamantly refused, he seriously examined his Christian faith. This quirk of fate propelled him toward a seminary. There he set his sights on the mission field, where he would be able to use his knowledge of audiovisual techniques. Doris Ove cut that dream short; she had had enough of out-of-the-way places. Ove's next goal was to preach interesting and exciting sermons using his acting talent and skills. During his religious internship he found many other areas of church work that he enjoyed as well. He entered the regular ordained ministry and, in his words, "never regretted my choice."

Almost fifty years after he left, Bob Ove revisited the Mescalero Apache Reservation, eager to take another look after the long hiatus. Whitetail was still scenic and serene, just as it was when the Chiricahuas lived there, but another dimension had been added: a serenity bordering on the sacred. Looking over the silent, broad expanse of wild grasses and tall, tall evergreens, Ove was filled with awe. The Whitetail forest had kept growing toward heaven while he had furthered his education in a Lutheran seminary and had preached in churches across America. Now retired from the ministry, he had the time to indulge in his favorite hobby—photography. Taking out his newest camera, he again snapped shots of Whitetail, a place once filled by the laughter of Chiricahua children, now home only to spirits and memories.

A different Mrs. Ove, Pat, accompanied Ove on his trip back to Whitetail in 1992. She watched him, as I did, react to the memories bouncing around in his head and heart and saw the changing expressions cross his face. In their private moments far away from the reservation, she must have shared more of his thoughts than are written in these recollections. For the rest of us, this book that describes the Chiricahua Apache community through the eyes of a teacher, at a time long past, will have to suffice. This book is a snapshot in words and photos of a time nearly fifty years ago, when few people from the outside world knew the Chiricahuas well, but when there lived among them individuals whose personal memories preserved a people's brave and tragic history. Ove recognized that he had come into the community completely ignorant of Apache history and culture, and that what he learned during his time among them constituted only a small fragment of their ancient culture. But he also believed that his personal observations, limited though they were, might help to preserve a small fragment of the history of Whitetail and to provide insight into the spirits of the remarkable people who became his students, neighbors, and in some cases friends.

Far down the mountain, in the village of Mescalero, Ove located some of his old students—grown now, of course, and some even grandparents. In talking with them, he decided to write a memoir about the days at Whitetail. No, he assured the Apaches, it would not be an anthropological treatise; his recollections were totally different. And it would not be a scholarly work, written from the outside looking in. This book would be written by someone who was close to their culture—a teacher who had lived among them at a specific time long past, a time when all Indian people were viewed differently than they are today. In the late 1940s Americans were not as sensitive to other cultures as they currently are, and certain of Ove's descriptions of life at Whitetail might, to some, appear insensitive. Not so; he is simply relating his experiences as he perceived them nearly fifty years ago.

This is Bob Ove's recollection, but it is the story of the friends, the descendants, and the other relatives of the Chiricahua Apaches—Geronimo's group—and about some of the descendants of the Warm Springs Apaches. Where the word "Apache" is used without any further distinction, rest assured that it refers to the Chiricahuas and the Warm Springs people only, and to no other Apache group.

A word about the title: The Chiricahua Apache kinship system is much more flexible and open-ended than the one with which most people are familiar. For example, Mildred I. Cleghorn, the former chairperson of the Fort Sill Chiricahua/Warm Springs Apache Tribe in Apache, Oklahoma, told me in private conversation: "As long as anyone has one drop of Chiricahua or Warm Springs blood, they are related to me. Only one drop will do it."

Cleghorn calls Kathleen Kanseah, a resident of the Mescalero Apache Reservation, her "cousin," and they are indeed kin. The relationship goes back in time to common ancestors, a woman named Go-lah-ah-tsa and her husband named Clee-neh. This couple were Ms. Cleghorn's paternal grandparents and Ms. Kanseah's paternal great-grandparents. Therefore, while they are not exactly "cousins," according to non-Apache cultural reckoning, they surely are related. But not all ancestors can be identified as easily. In some cases, when Chiricahua children prisoners of war were sent to school, they were given Anglicized names, and through time their original names have long been forgotten. I had an interesting experience in helping one Chiricahua woman trace her heritage. Her grandmother was given an "American" name either by the soldiers or by government officials, and she asked me to carefully look for this name in documents found during research. I hoped to find a reference somewhere, but I was not optimistic. Some years later I found a letter from interpreter George Wratten to Carlisle School Superintendent Richard Henry Pratt urging Pratt to return this pupil to the prison camp to care for her ailing relatives. Wratten wrote the student's Anglicized name and, immediately following, added her Chiricahua name in parentheses. I brought back a copy of that letter and gave it to my friend. It was quite a touching moment.

Many Chiricahua elders know who their relatives are, usually because they have been told by their parents and grandparents. However, there is no guarantee that this information will be carried into the future, given the speedy acculturation and assimilation taking place and the eagerness of many young people to disregard their roots.

Nonetheless, at least one available document lists Chiricahua relations. Gillett Griswold, in his unpublished 1970 genealogical compendium entitled "The Fort Sill Apaches: Their Vital Statistics, Tribal Origins, Antecedents," recorded the bloodlines with help from numerous Chiricahuas, including Ms. Cleghorn. It is true that some of the connections conflict with others, but patient readers of this one-hundred-fifty-page description—a rare manuscript now under lock and key at the Fort Sill (Oklahoma) Museum—will be rewarded with a general idea of Chiricahua kinship. The manuscript, however, is not structured in an academic, anthropological framework. Rather, it is simply an alphabetized catalog of names with narratives, when possible, of consanguinity.

As Chiricahua and Warm Springs Apaches, the children at the Whitetail Day School were directly and indirectly related to Geronimo, even though many of them did not literally share his blood. In the days when the Apaches were free, intermingling characterized their way of life. For example, although born into the Bedonkohe band, by the 1850s Geronimo and others of his group had joined the Mimbres Apache group headed by Mangas Coloradas. A decade later he was living with Cochise and the Chiricahuas, probably having married a Chiricahua woman, She-ga, by that time.

Most of the Whitetail children's parents and grandparents knew the warrior, were related to him, or had ridden with him in the past. But not all held him in high esteem; some blamed their incarceration on his stubborn reluctance to surrender. Although feelings ran high in either direction, it is certain that every child in the day school at Whitetail had heard stories at home about the famous warrior's escapades. And no doubt many of them were proud to be Geronimo's kids.

H. Henrietta Stockel
Rio Rancho, New Mexico

Acknowledgments

When I opened my Christmas gifts just before my retirement from the pulpit in December, 1991, I found a copy of H. Henrietta Stockel's book *Women of the Apache Nation: Voices of Truth*. I had been telling my wife, Pat, that now that I was free of ministerial duties, I wanted to spend some time writing my memoirs for the kids; I really thought no one else would be interested. She gave me Henrietta's book to prod my memories of a time more than forty years earlier when I started my first real job out of college as a day school teacher on the Mescalero Apache Reservation in New Mexico.

Pat also gave me a video, *Geronimo and the Apache Resistance*. When we viewed it the next day, I could see that the gray-haired, stocky narrator, a man of about fifty, was obviously an Apache. What really excited me was his name: Berle Kanseah. Berle had been a pupil in my fifth and sixth grades at Whitetail, on the reservation, all those years ago. When I was incredulous, Pat pointed out that since Berle had been about ten years old when I was there, he really would be about fifty by now.

My enthusiasm faded temporarily two weeks later when my wife became ill. In those tense days when she was undergoing tests and having surgery, I began to read Henrietta's book to keep my mind busy. Again, I was pleasantly surprised to find the names of people I had known years before. I used my brother-in-law's computer to record some memories. Then one day after I had finished reading her book, I dropped Henrietta a line to let her know how fascinating I found her work and why I had a particular interest in it. A few days later I was amazed to find a lengthy reply from her in my mail. This led to another round of letters and an invitation to join her on the Mescalero Apache Reservation in July of that year (1992) for the annual puberty rites celebration. She even made reservations for my wife and me in Ruidoso, the closest off-reservation town.

My return after all those years was both gratifying and heartbreaking: gratifying to see old friends, but heartbreaking to hear how many of my little kids were deceased—quite a few from alcoholism. In my mind they were still the cute little black-haired, black-eyed cherubs I had taught so long ago. Before that visit was over, Henrietta had talked me into writing this book, offering all her considerable skill and experience as a respected author and authority in the field. I was both encouraged and flattered by her offer, but I had no way of realizing then how much pain and struggle I would experience dredging up those memories.

My thanks to Henrietta for being my mentor, editor, encourager, and friend. All I had to do was pour out my memories on paper. She arranged them, inserted important background information on each of the people I knew, and placed them in their historical setting. Henrietta is one of a very select group of writers who have made the Chiricahua Apache nation their central subject of interest. Most of those writers have now passed on; only a handful remain. This is strange in light of the universal recognition of the Chiricahua Apaches, and especially of Geronimo. My profound thanks to her for helping me shed a tiny spot of light on the people who once made headlines from one end of this country to the other.

My special thanks go to Berle Kanseah for the hours he sacrificed to reopen the doors to bygone days when we were teacher and pupil in the little school at Whitetail. He also opened his heart to me, sharing his feelings about the many changes that have taken place on the reservation over the years. Thanks to Berle's wife, Lynette, for keeping up the correspondence and making me feel so welcome in their home. Many thanks to Lynette's mother, Dorcie Kazhe, for helping me reminisce and for offering me shelter on my subsequent visits to the reservation. During these times she filled me in on some happenings to my Whitetail "family" over the years I had been away.

The "kids" I talked with gave me their valuable time, some even taking off from their jobs to recall the old days. Vernon Simmons, for example, spent several days reminiscing with me over breakfast.

Thanks to Mescalero Apache Chairman Wendell Chino, whom I first met when he was a young Dutch Reformed pastor at the mission during my days at Whitetail. He still serves the Lord, although in a different way.

"Now," he said, "as the tribal leader, I'm serving all the people of the Mescalero Apache Reservation, not just those of my denomination."

Pastor Robert Schut of the First Reformed Church and Father Tom Herbst, O.F.M., of Saint Joseph's Mission, gave me helpful insights on the cultural changes (and the things that haven't changed!) over the years since I left.

It was good to learn through correspondence that Bernice TenHaken, wife of the Dutch Reformed pastor during my years on the reservation, and the former principal, Lonnie Hardin, were still alive and well. Their letters and encouragement were a help to me in this project.

Art Blazer and the Landries plugged a great many gaps in my memory and gave me a chance to renew treasured friendships.

There are many others, on and off the reservation, who helped me check through a myriad of details and fragmented memories. I don't have the phenomenal memory that Apaches are blessed with, so my mind needed much prodding. That they remembered me at all amazed me, but that their memories of me were as pleasant as mine were of them was a heartwarming discovery.

I must repeat my indebtedness to my dear wife, Pat, who started the whole process. I am especially appreciative of her encouragement through the many hours and days and weeks of labor at the computer or in the darkroom when she was a "book" widow.

Reverend Robert S. Ove
Cheyenne, Wyoming

When Bob Ove and I first met in Ruidoso, I had no idea we would become co-authors. In our previous telephone calls, he and had I discussed our mutual interest in the Chiricahua Apaches and especially in Whitetail, their high mountain home on the Mescalero Apache Reservation from 1913 to the middle of the 1950s. I had written two books about the Chiricahuas and two others as well, but I never expected to embark on a writing expedition with a minister who lived almost one thousand miles to the north in Cheyenne, Wyoming. After only three days together and one flat tire on the way down the mountain from a visit to Whitetail, I knew we would write a unique book.

Bob Ove, or "the Rev," as I began to call him, has a distinctive story to tell. He taught the descendants of Geronimo's band of Chiricahuas, and other Apache children as well, at Whitetail from 1948 to 1950, a time when some of the aging sons and daughters of the great Apache leaders were still alive and in daily contact with him. He heard their stories and looked into the eyes of their grandchildren, staring back at him in a classroom. Clearly, many of the youngsters were not interested in book learning, but the Rev persisted and, in the process managed to get some of his points across, often through innovative and unorthodox methods. Some of those children overcame extraordinary obstacles in life and are adults now; many still live on the Mescalero Apache Reservation and were delighted to be reunited with their former teacher. Oral history and oral tradition have finally acquired credibility, and that is fortunate; otherwise Ove's recollections would be looked on as mere memories. Instead, he and I have produced a document that combines both oral schools. No one else has chronicled Chiricahua Apache history from this perspective. And I am blessed to have been part of it because of the Rev's conviction that I would represent with accuracy and honesty the portion of his life lived at our beloved Whitetail. I cannot thank him and Pat enough for their trust in my abilities.

I tip my hat and curtsy deeply to Louise d'A. Fairchild, who is always there for me, no matter what the cost, the prize, or the pain. I would not be able to write without her support and understanding. With each book we finish, we embark on another, almost with no hesitation, so she is as involved in my writing as I am.

To the Chiricahua Apaches who have been my friends and family through the years especially, and to the other pals who have nothing at all to do with Indians, thanks a lot.

Always, with arms upraised to the Creator, *'ixehe*.

H. Henrietta Stockel
Rio Rancho, New Mexico

Introduction

Where had these giant pines come from? I stared at them in wonder and spoke aloud as I poked along a lonely dirt road at Whitetail, an abandoned settlement about eight thousand feet high in the forest on the Mescalero Apache Reservation in southeastern New Mexico. The July morning sun felt good on my aging bones and seemed to dry up some of the humidity, but thunderclouds rumbled in the distance, and the sky to the west was darkening. The wet season in this part of the Southwest occurs in midsummer, and storms frequently roll in, dump their heavy load of refreshing rainwater, and move on, all in a matter of minutes. I breathed deeply and took in the unique aroma of a wet forest, like no other smell on earth. Beneath the heavy odor I thought I smelled more rain riding in on the wind, which had picked up quite a bit in just the last few seconds. It seemed a good time to head for cover under the trees at the side of the road.

As I waited there, a flood of bittersweet memories washed over me. The pines that protected me from the sudden storm now overshadowed the tiny masonry-and-stucco home where I had once lived, right next to the schoolhouse. These days the tall pines probably keep the residence quite cool, which was my purpose in planting them more than forty years ago when they—and I—were saplings.

Since that time a whole way of life has vanished in America; with it went a segment of history that has never been recorded. As a young teacher in the government day school at Whitetail back in the days when the reservation community was thriving, I was privileged to live and work among the Chiricahua Apaches known popularly as Geronimo's "band" and their descendants.[1] The older folks in the community were the survivors of nearly three decades of imprisonment by the U.S. government.

Among those who spoke no English was the great Apache warrior Dahteste, who was known to everyone in the community as "Old Lady Coonie," and who lived with her niece, Eliza. Along with another woman warrior named Lozen, Dahteste was responsible for initiating the surrender negotiations that led to the incarceration. I remember Dahteste riding along the dirt road on the back of her burro, clip-clopping slowly to wherever she was going. She was never in a hurry. One day Eliza appeared with a shiny new pickup truck, and the burro was no longer needed for transportation. But he hung around for a long while, taking it easy out in the rolling field that separated the Coonie house from the Istee place.

The Istee family at Whitetail were direct descendants of Chief Victorio, one of the most famous of the Warm Springs Apache leaders. Charles Istee, son of the great chief, became my friend, and we spent many hours together in conversation. The Istee house, when I last saw it, was somewhat intact compared with the other homes at Whitetail, and it brings back many memories each time I see it and other evidences of my years among the Chiricahua Apaches.

Pieces of Eliza Coonie's truck, parked for more than forty years, remain today in that now overgrown field between her house and the Istee home, rusting and sinking into the soft Whitetail earth. Oddly, a headlight is shiny, and its chrome gleams even in the rain. Not much else survives of the Coonie house; the walls have collapsed inward and outward, but a rusty old metal water trough sits in front, full of treasures: leather baby shoes, Irby Kazhe's old metal lunch pail, his name still etched on the lid, rusting double bedsprings, and the other residue of a life lived simply and honestly, but in poverty.

Gone now are all of the two- and four-room wooden houses and barns built at Whitetail around 1913 and 1914 by the government especially for the newly released Chiricahua prisoners of war. The houses were so poorly constructed that they could not withstand for long the rigors and vagaries of high altitude and mountain climate, and they disintegrated under the pressure of the long, wet, and very cold winters. Their replacements, constructed about 1938, fared a little better, at least until the 1950s, when folks began leaving the area for reservation housing located closer to the agency headquarters and community services. Like their predecessors, these houses are today dissolving into the beautiful landscape. In less than a decade nothing will remain, except perhaps the two masonry-and-stucco houses and the school.

When the rain shower let up, I peeked through a window frame, minus the glass, into my old classroom. It had become a storage barn for hay; the children's desks and seats were gone forever. I should not have been surprised at the trashed interior, but I was; it saddened me. For a second I thought I could hear the Apache kids laughing at me, the white man teacher they called "Indah," after they had played another trick on me. But I imagined sounds that did not really sound like laughter. Perhaps, although he had never come to Whitetail while he was alive, the spirit of Geronimo was flying around.

Geronimo was always in favor of education for the Chiricahua children and showed his dedication openly when the Apaches were prisoners of war at Mount Vernon, Alabama, from 1887 to 1894. He patrolled the aisles of the one-room classroom and kept order by waving a willow switch back and forth over the pupils' heads. No one dared misbehave, and doubtless the youngsters learned their lessons well.

Chiricahua Apache children have a long history of being schooled by the "white man." It began in 1886, when they and their families were prisoners of war. More than five hundred men, women, and children were incarcerated at two Florida sites: Fort Marion, in St. Augustine, and Fort Pickens, on Santa Rosa Island. Although the military had no compunction about confining the adults, holding innocent children posed a sticky set of problems. While vigilant national Indian rights watchdog groups hovered closely, the government quickly decided to educate captive Apache youth in the ways of the dominant culture.

The youngest were placed in the charge of the Sisters of Saint Joseph, who lived in a convent about ten minutes' walk from Fort Marion. Initially, the nuns spent about an hour and a half each morning with the children. They organized them and marched them down the concrete steps from the fort's parapet, where the tipis were pitched, into casemates abutting the courtyard. The sisters thought that simple lessons could be taught without distraction in those dark caverns. A few months later the government and the sisters reached an agreement that allowed the nuns to continue instructing the children, but away from the fort. It had become increasingly difficult to teach the kids because their parents wanted to participate too, particularly their fearsome warrior-fathers, who stood in the rear and commented in Apache—and even learned to sing the simple songs the nuns taught the children. The young nuns were naturally intimidated.

Being a good businesswoman, the convent's Mother Superior requested payments of twenty to forty dollars per month per child, depending on the grade, to teach the twenty-six girls and forty-two boys. Government negotiators refused, held firm, and offered a paltry seven-fifty per child, plus a condition: the total sum for one year of teaching all the Apache children remaining at Fort Marion must not exceed nine hundred dollars.[2] The nuns reluctantly agreed, and the arrangement was formalized.

Instead of having lessons at the fort, the children now walked to the convent for their instructions, chaperoned by young nuns. On the way, the children skipped and fussed and behaved like any other group of youngsters. At the convent they crowded into a bathhouse to change their clothes before frolicking in the ocean, watched closely by the sisters. Later, when they were taken into church for their academic lessons, "like electricity, they jumped from bench to bench, so educating these children was not just a matter of teaching the ABCs," said Sister Mary Albert, the convent's historian. "Their mental health [exemplified by good behavior] was also important. The mingling of these children with people from another culture broke down resistance. Because they were cooped up at the fort, walking to the convent also gave them some sense of freedom, as did the interaction between the younger nuns and the Apache children."[3]

Not as fortunate were the youngsters' older brothers and sisters. On October 23, 1886, not long after arrival from the Southwest, ninety-five boys and girls were selected by the military overseers to be taken from their families and sent to Carlisle Indian Industrial School, in Carlisle, Pennsylvania, located approximately ten miles southwest of Harrisburg. Five older boys who had been imprisoned at Fort Pickens with warriors from bands led by Naiche, Geronimo, and Mangus were added to that group, bringing its size up to one hundred. In April, 1887, another sixty-two Chiricahua children said good-bye to their heartsick families and started on the long journey by sea from Florida to New York and then overland to Pennsylvania, where tragedy in the form of loneliness and disease awaited them.

In the early history of the thirteen colonies, Carlisle had been the site of a frontier military post. During the Revolutionary War a number of Hessian prisoners were incarcerated there. In July, 1863, the post was shelled in the Battle of Gettysburg. The burned buildings were rebuilt in 1865, but the site was abandoned in the early 1870s. In 1879 the old post was donated to the Department of the Interior to serve as an educational establishment for Indians. The first group, eighty-two young Sioux, arrived on October 6, 1879. Forty-seven Kiowas, Cheyennes, and Pawnees appeared the following month. Seven years later the school's superintendent, Capt. Richard Henry Pratt, solicited the government's permission to move the older Chiricahua children from Fort Marion to Carlisle.

Richard Imach was one of the children chosen to go. Years later he told his daughter Mildred Cleghorn, long-time Chairperson (now retired) of the Fort Sill Chiricahua/Warm Springs Apache Tribe in Apache, Oklahoma, about the selection process. The boys were lined up in the sand on the beach below the fort, not in any special order. Because the children's ages were unknown, the selection was based on height. The boy next to Richard was as tall as he was but ground his feet into the sand to appear shorter. He was bypassed, temporarily, while Richard, standing tall as a proud young Chiricahua, was picked and sent off to Carlisle.

When they arrived at the school, the boys and girls were immediately separated. The children had their hair cut, they were forced to put on trousers and dresses, and they were lined up and given names. Legend has it that the children were divided by sex and placed in rows of twenty-six, arranged according to height. The tallest was then given a name that started with A; the shortest got a name beginning with Z. Many descendants of those children still carry the names today; quite a few contemporary Chiricahuas have no idea what their ancestors' real Apache names were.

The first lessons in English actually began at mealtimes with the children learning how to pronounce the names of utensils and food. The older and larger Apache kids were expected to assist the smaller ones beside them. Tiny James Kaywaykla, the youngest Apache at Carlisle, sat next to Asa Daklugie, the largest, and one of the oldest children there. The extent of the small boy's fright and loneliness is illustrated in an anecdote recorded by author Eve Ball. Asa Daklugie told her that one Sunday morning at breakfast he was passing hotcakes from left to right. Kaywaykla, who was sitting on his right, was the last served, but there was still plenty on the plate. When the maple syrup reached him, however, the jar was empty. James turned the pitcher upside down and only a few drops ran out. He began to cry, a most unusual reaction in an Apache of any age. "It was the first time that I'd seen one of the Apache children [cry]," Daklugie said. "I felt sorry for him. . . . It was against the rule, but I got more of that maple syrup." Then something else happened. Said Daklugie, "The boy who brought it asked if I knew that Kanseah was in the hospital. . . . That was terrible news, for nearly every Apache taken there had died."[4]

The student waiter was referring to Jasper Kanseah, an orphaned nephew of Geronimo, who was thirteen when his uncle's band surrendered. Being one of the lucky ones and blessed with a very strong body and mind, Kanseah did not die from tuberculosis. He never forgot the importance of his experiences at Carlisle. For the rest of his long life he insisted that his children and grandchildren obtain a proper education so that they could effectively and comfortably compete in the white world.

This was consistent with the course of study at Carlisle, as described in its catalogue: "It is the aim of the Carlisle school to train the Indian youth of both sexes to take upon themselves the duties of citizenship. Indian young men and young women are given thorough academic and industrial training, which prepares them to earn a living, either among their own people or away from the reservation in competition with whites."[5] Among the subjects offered in addition to basic academic courses were agriculture, business, boys' industries such as blacksmithing and tailoring, and girls' household arts that included cooking, laundering, and sewing.

One enhancement of Indian education at Carlisle that caught the government's approval was a program that Superintendent Pratt called the "outing system." Each pupil at the school was expected to spend at least one year in a nearby farm home, applying the lessons learned in the classroom and performing a number of tasks for the family. For example, an Apache girl was expected to help cook, wash the clothes, and do the family's mending. Pupils participating in Carlisle's outing program were paid one dollar to fifteen dollars per month, in proportion to the kind of work they did and the ability and skill they showed in doing it. The students' earnings were deposited in individual bank accounts and were accessible to them for purchasing necessities. Many families became quite fond of the students and kept in touch with them long after they had returned to their natural parents. In turn, to show their respect and gratitude, a few Apache children adopted the first or last names of their local families.

Pratt's outing system received a great deal of support in Congress, and similar programs were started in Indian schools from Oregon to Indian Territory. However, due to politics, local customs, external influences, and unavoidable abuses, not all of the programs were successful. The concept failed, for example, in certain areas of the West, where the cheap labor that Indian students could provide was more important than integrating them into white society.

Another factor that influenced the success or failure of a given outing system was the vitality of the children participating in it. Tuberculosis was everywhere in those days, indiscriminately infecting its victims. Healthy and unhealthy students alike were sent out to local homes, regardless of the danger to them and their host families. In many instances, the farm family had members who were already sick, and the deadly contagion flourished. Usually, when a healthy pupil entered a home where others were sick, that student fell ill. When the period of education at Carlisle was at long last over, at least thirty-seven Chiricahua Apache children had died from contagious diseases acquired at the school and through participating in the outing system. Many others not in danger of dying nevertheless suffered for the rest of their lives.

When the mournful barking of a lonesome dog came up at me from the broken-out basement windows and brought me back to reality, I realized that I was trespassing. My stomach churned. Suddenly, I was eager to get out of there, lest another human being should appear, if only to feed the dog, whose nose was full of porcupine quills.

It had been six years since my last visit to Whitetail, my only visit in the thirty-five years that had passed since I left. I remembered driving the dirt road in 1986 at a snail's pace toward the one house that still looked habitable. Sure enough, an older, graying Apache man heard the engine and stepped out with a gang of children around him. He stared at me, and I introduced myself, hastily explaining why I was intruding. He said he was Leroy Coonie. Immediately I remembered a handsome young man who used to stop at my house every now and then during my two-year tenure at Whitetail. Finally I saw the light of recognition in his eyes, too, and we talked. When I returned six years later, in 1992, I learned that he had killed his first wife. The much younger woman I had seen with him during a 1986 visit had also died in the interim. By that time, forty-four years had passed from the time I first arrived, and practically nothing—and no one—was left at Whitetail.

Geronimo's Kids

Chapter 1
Remembering Whitetail

The Mescalero Apache Reservation was formally established by Executive Order of President Ulysses S. Grant in 1873. Unlike other Indian reservations in the desert Southwest, Mescalero sits high above the earth's floor and is surrounded by fragrant pines and other trees, homes to many species of birds. It has snow in winter and shade in summer. The streams run cold and clear, providing nourishing, sweet water to wildlife of many varieties. I had never heard of it in 1948 when I was at the end of my third year at Carthage College, twelve credits short of my B.A. degree. The school offered only six credit hours for the summer session. If I stayed at Carthage for summer school, I would still need another six hours—another semester—to fulfill the requirements for graduation.

Being a restless sort, I did not want to sit around a classroom any longer than necessary, so I searched for a school that offered twelve or more credits in its summer session. Most of the schools I found were too expensive, and others were difficult for various reasons, but I finally discovered Arizona State University, in Tempe, where I could complete all twelve credit hours during the summer. But another, more complicated problem arose and I felt as though I could not win: I would have to wait a year before getting my degree in education.

Needless to say, that was a big stumbling block to finding a job. There were other obstacles in my way as well. There was a surplus of English teachers at the secondary level. If I had qualified in physical education or one of the sciences, I could have had my pick of jobs; unfortunately, those areas were not my strengths. And then, every state required its teachers to offer courses in state history and government, subjects that could not be learned on the job. At the beginning of August, 1948, very few teaching posts were vacant, and I was at a loss.

As summer drew to a close, I searched frantically for work. One day a friend came back to the dorm with the exciting news that the government was looking for teachers to work on Indian reservations. Since there seemed to be no other jobs, I decided to investigate the opportunity and took the long bus ride to Phoenix, where the Bureau of Indian Affairs (BIA) was located. In those days, one BIA agency building housed all the operations for the southwestern reservations. After brief introductions, the regional superintendent, who had the enthusiasm of a used car salesman, showed me a wall papered with photos of area scenery and Indian faces from the many reservations under his authority. "Where would you like to go?" he asked. Having had enough of the southwestern desert, I expressed a preference for mountains and cool, wooded hills. He nodded sympathetically, aware of the trials of summer in Arizona. With a pointy forefinger he jabbed at a group of photos. "What about the Mescalero Apaches?" he asked. "This place is over seven thousand feet high, up in the tall timbers. It's one of our most scenic spots." I agreed excitedly. Here, luckily, was my first job as a teacher.

In those days the Bureau of Indian Affairs did not require state certification, so I was eligible to teach. My problems seemed to have disappeared. Within a few days I was on a bus headed for the Mescalero Apache Reservation to have a look around. We pulled into the reservation's "downtown,"—one store and a post office—at two o'clock in the morning. The first thing I discovered was that it is a good deal cooler in the high country than on the desert floor. Next, I noticed that there were no motels. I stood shivering in the dark morning mountain air, a young man, green as grass, and alone on an Apache Indian reservation, looking into the distance at the disappearing red taillights of the bus.

And then I saw it—a sign of life in the blackness. A small wink of light shone from a window far above me. As my eyes grew accustomed to the dark, I realized that the town of Mescalero, small as it was, was built on a series of terraces; the lighted window was on the third level. By the time I arrived at the door, the light was out. I made a fist and banged repeatedly, hoping the occupants were not asleep. At long last a big hulk of a man in pajamas opened the door and invited me in. "We can talk later," he said in a loud whisper as he ushered me into an upstairs guest room. I was so exhausted that I collapsed fully clothed onto the hard horsehair mattress and pulled a scratchy woolen blanket up to my chin. Somewhere around here was my new home, but at that moment I really did not care.

In the morning the big man in pajamas and bare feet stood next to a frazzle-haired woman in a robe. She was heating something on an ancient stove. A boy of about ten years sat at the table. They all greeted me with warm smiles. "I'm Harvey TeBeast and this is my wife and son," he said. As I explained myself, Harvey put in front of me a badly chipped china bowl containing a thin stew. One slice of bread in the center soaked up the juices, half hiding a potato slice trapped under one corner. Along with encouraging me to have another helping, Harvey told me that he was working with his cousin, the Dutch Reformed church's pastor, and that they were building a new addition on the church. "This is God's country," Harvey added.

Later that morning I met Lonnie Hardin, principal of the Mescalero school and my supervisor, and learned right off that the Indian service had been his life and career since his college days. Before coming to Mescalero he had taught a tribe that lived at the bottom of the Grand Canyon and could get in and out only by mule, and he thought Mescalero, a community of about seventy-five people settled around the tribal agency, was the big city. Coming from the Phoenix area, I naturally thought differently, but I said little as we drove through some of the most breathtaking scenery I had ever seen. Our destination was Whitetail, a community another thousand feet higher up the mountain, which had been without a teacher for about a year.

At the second cattle guard on the right of the main road we reached the turnoff to the Chiricahua Apache settlement and drove on gravel for the next seventeen miles. The road was just wide enough for two cars to pass if they slowed down. Our vehicle snaked its way between the endless pines, climbing through the forest until we reached a switchback where the road sloped away sharply on both sides. Then the road made an abrupt turn into the last, very steep climb, forcing Lonnie to downshift his Lincoln Zephyr a couple of gears. I was relieved at the slower pace. My host's driving was terrifying me, and anxiety was churning my intestines. As this fearless fellow traveled at full throttle through hair-raising turns, he would look me straight in the eye as he talked, disregarding the road.

The terrain leveled out after we passed what was known locally as the Whitetail summit, and when we reached the unofficial center of the settlement, the schoolhouse, the road widened a bit. Lonnie pointed out a cozy little house, called a "teacherage," right next to the empty school. I remember that it looked good to someone who had no other prospects for the future—damned good.

Reflecting the morality of the day, in the late 1940s the Bureau of Indian Affairs would not send an unmarried man to an isolated spot like Whitetail on the Mescalero Apache Reservation. That policy was set in concrete; there were no exceptions. Had I been a carefree bachelor, the job of teaching the Chiricahua children would have gone to someone else. Fortunately, I was engaged to a young woman from Chicago, and after many long-distance conversations I somehow convinced her that starting married life with me in a remote Indian community in New Mexico was just what she had always wanted to do. It took a lot of heartfelt effort, including pleading, but she finally saw things my way, and I traveled to Chicago for the wedding. We had a one-night honeymoon in my parents' bedroom, then packed and prepared for a long train ride to the reservation. Three days later, after spending the first several days of wedded bliss sitting up in a railroad coach, we detrained about a mile west of Tularosa, New Mexico. The only public transportation into that small town was by bus, but the bus ran only once a day, and we had already missed it. A U.S. mail truck was going our way, though, so we climbed aboard. My bride rode in the cab while I reclined unceremoniously among the mail sacks. We were able to find a bus from Tularosa to the reservation, and the next day, after spending a pleasant recuperative night with the Hardins discussing my new post, Mr. Hardin chauffeured us on the last leg of our adventure to Whitetail.

My young bride, a city girl, ooh'd and aah'd at the magnificent scenery, and truly it was even more beautiful than I had remembered it from my first visit. The fields were alive with yellow flowers as we approached Dark Canyon, and then we saw the spectacular sight of Sierra Blanca, the sacred high peak of the Apaches, framed in the canyon; it seemed to float above the thick forest. But reality began to set in as we turned off at the unmarked cattle guard and climbed mile after mile up the narrow gravel road. Finally cresting the summit, we began passing the humble dwellings of the locals, and then the school came into view, a yellow oasis in a green sea of grass and pines. This would be home for the next two years, and I was suddenly concerned about how my wife would accept the situation after the rush of romance and excitement wore off. The environment and the remoteness, as appealing as they were to many people, could be intimidating to urbanites. I was hoping that Doris wouldn't throw up her hands and run away screaming (though she would never get far without a car). But she seemed to accept the situation with stoicism, partly, I suppose, because of the grit and self-discipline she had inherited from her parents.

We shared a sinking feeling when Mr. Hardin left our drive and sped off down the road in a cloud of dust. We went into our new home to look around. The house was already completely furnished. We brought just our clothes and my books and a few odds and ends; everything fit into a couple of packing boxes and a few old suitcases that had easily nestled into the trunk of Hardin's car. Later my old college steamer trunk arrived with bedding, more clothes, and a few wedding gifts.

A perfect square, our house had four rooms and a bath. The living room was practically fifteen feet by twelve or thirteen feet. Each of the two bedrooms was perhaps nine or ten feet square with closets sharing the inside wall. The one that shared the front wall of the house with the living room became my study. The tiny bathroom, set between the other bedroom and the kitchen, contained a tub, stool, and sink. There was barely enough room in it for one person. A brick chimney ran up between the bathroom and kitchen walls. It was a blessing in the cold, cold winters, but its extreme warmth caused many problems later, including a fire during our second week at Whitetail.

All the basic furniture, even the living room rug, had been supplied by the Bureau of Indian Affairs. The bureau provided a couch and an overstuffed chair to sit on in the living room. We later added a phonograph, a pair of end tables, and a touch of class: yellow plastic curtains ordered from the Montgomery Ward catalog.

A double bed almost filled the master bedroom, leaving just enough room for one dresser, but that seemed to be enough. We had not brought much in the way of clothing, but we still had more than the average Whitetail resident.

The study contained a single bed, a desk filled with BIA paper, pencils, pens, and carbon paper, and a rather stiff wooden chair. I built a bookcase on both sides and over the top of the desk to accommodate my growing library.

The kitchen was about seven feet wide and nine feet long. It had a gas stove on one side and kitchen cabinets full of BIA cookware, dishes, and silverware on the other side. At one end stood a drop-leaf table with four chairs tucked in. A card table could be set up in the living room to provide for overflow guests.

Appended to the house were two porches. The one at the front of the house was about eight or ten feet wide and stood out about six feet from the wall. Here we relaxed on warm evenings and entertained visitors. Two posts supported the roof, and a flight of three or four concrete steps provided access from the porch up to the living room door. Down the stairs and to the right on the lawn sat a dilapidated wooden box in which the fire hose was coiled.

The other porch, on the kitchen side of the house, faced the school. A twenty-square-foot propane refrigerator with two large doors occupied a portion of this area; it was so efficient that it froze everything solid in short order. Every now and then we had to remove the milk, soda pop, and other liquids so they wouldn't burst their containers. In winter, which was ordinarily long and cold at Whitetail, these same items were removed and placed on the porch, in nature's refrigerator. A storage area for mops, a vacuum cleaner, and other household appliances shared the kitchen porch, as did stairs with a safety railing leading down to the basement. The porch was enclosed with screening impregnated with a newfangled translucent plastic that was supposed to keep the wind from howling through. The concrete floor flowed out the door and down the five or six side steps. A few of the Apache men liked to sit on these steps in the sun and tell stories. In the backyard I built a doghouse with a penthouse on its roof for the cats.

The basement of the teacherage housed a workbench equipped with power tools for the community's use. The Apaches themselves seemed to have only the most rudimentary implements, and they had practically no place to store them. Opposite the workbench, at the other end of the basement, was an old coal bin that I converted into a darkroom. Next to the darkroom was the furnace and water heater. Heat from the furnace vented up into an outlet located at the very center of the upstairs living area. The grate that covered the outlets was flush with the living room floor and had to be crossed to get to the bathroom and the master bedroom.

Everything in the teacherage and the school except the lights and smaller appliances ran on propane from a large tank in the backyard. Also out there were the clothesline and the trash drums. If wild animals did not dispose of the contents first, the remains of foodstuffs and other household debris were burned on the spot in the drums and then hauled off to the dump.

It did not take long to put all our belongings away, and then we went outside for a look around. The great feeling of peace at Whitetail began to penetrate our bones as the ring of travel subsided from our ears. Time seemed to stand still. When the initial enchantment with the environment and our circumstances wore off, we began to realize just how sequestered Whitetail really was. One dirt road, impassable in inclement weather, connected us with the main agency buildings far down the mountain. Seventy-five individuals were employed there, mostly Mescalero Apaches. It was a long, long trip to get groceries or to visit anyone in town.

Being surrounded by a totally different culture and unfamiliar customs made us a bit uncomfortable at first. It would have been a lot harder for us, though, without the school's cooks and bus drivers, who patiently explained Chiricahua Apache etiquette, particularly the long wait I often had to endure until someone speaking to me had finished talking. Chiricahuas tend to speak slowly and frequently think between sentences. They knew this about each other, and it was not unusual to see two people carrying on a conversation with both saying nothing for periods of time. But I was very uncomfortable with standing beside someone and waiting for that individual to continue talking or to reintroduce a theme. Being immediately immersed in the culture helped us adjust more quickly, I believe, and everyone was very patient with us. They had endured so much Western culture that they were more prepared for us than we were for them.

The first community activity I recall was a reception which, I believe, took place at the church. The Chiricahuas gave speeches for our benefit and presented gifts to us. During the refreshments almost every member of the community came forth and personally welcomed us. At that point I got my first hint of the great Apache sense of humor. I heard a great deal of laughter, which at first I thought was probably their way of covering up discomfort; there may have been some of that, but later I was caught up in it. At times it reminded me of Danish (my background) humor in which the storyteller must not laugh until the audience catches the point. Yes, I was the butt of some of the Apache giggles; but since I did not understand the language or the customs, I could only guess at what they found funny by reading the expressions on their faces and their surreptitious glances. And I never did find out what the joke was.

We also attended a reception down the mountain in Mescalero where we met the teachers and other government staff and learned that we belonged to two families: the Whitetail group and the civil service employee bunch. When this realization soaked in, we felt more comfortable.

As we traveled around the community and learned who lived in which house, Whitetail came to seem more and more crowded. People lived everywhere we looked. They were pushing back the trees for farmland, and even the cows and horses were an important part of the population. The people came to us one or two at a time, usually to get water or use the telephone or for some other purpose, then stayed to socialize. I can only remember one family who came just for a friendly visit. The teacherage was the source of water and gas, the entertainment center, the telephone exchange, the transportation station, a first-aid unit, and even a first court of adjudication when marital problems arose. Before long we also became a secondary grocery store and a snack bar; I began to order nonperishables by the case.

Charlie Istee came over once to check out an old horse-drawn plow that was languishing at the school. I discovered that the older Whitetail residents often used such antiques because it was cheaper to do the work themselves than to hire the community tractor and driver. The money they saved left the thrifty Apaches with extra income after the crops were sold. Charlie often stayed and spun his tales for me. I think he wanted to impress me with his lineage as the son of Chief Victorio. He succeeded, and he no doubt laughed at me when he went home or when he told Dahteste about me.

My wife and I were invited to enter very few homes other than those of Robert Geronimo and Hugh Chee. Most of my meetings with the families of the children took place at the school, but if I did stop at someone's house, the inhabitants would meet me on the porch and we would stand outside and chat. They were friendly enough, but then they rarely entered my house, either.

I found the remoteness of Whitetail refreshing and not as restricting as I had first feared. That germ of confidence came in handy as time went by, especially since I felt responsible for introducing my wife to this totally different life, far from the conveniences of urban life.

There were minor obstacles to be overcome immediately. The usual methods of cooking at sea level that Doris knew so well did not work at Whitetail. For example, boiling water at eight thousand feet was not the same as boiling water at sea level. We often stood in front of the stove and watched the water bubble away, looking as if it were actually 180 degrees, but it felt almost cool when we dipped in our fingers. Cooking instructions that worked at sea level produced raw or half-cooked food in the mountains. Changing her timing was not difficult, but Doris also had to learn to carve cuts of raw, bloody meat from huge chunks of freshly butchered beef just lowered off a dangerous, mean-looking hook. A chicken dinner started with catching and killing a live bird and then plucking it, chores she detested. On wash days, this brave young city woman, never complaining, lugged sacks of our dirty clothes over to the only washing machine available, which was located on the school grounds. The ten-year-old, round, top-loading machine had to be watched so that it did not pull the cord out of the wall as it danced across the floor with a full load. To make matters worse, the wringer that hung from the washer's side loved to shred clothing. Six months after we arrived, when I lost a pair of new pajamas to its appetite, I finally took revenge and chopped off the wringer with an ax. A replacement from some other section of the reservation worked satisfactorily.

Water was a continuing problem. Whitetail's supply was in a big tank next to the windmill. Both structures sat on a knoll north of the main road and about a mile east of the school. Normally Bill Landrie, another of Whitetail's Anglo inhabitants, kept the water running, but when he was at the cow camp it was my job to service the well. I would drive out past his home (the largest house in the community) and the church and turn north. The tank stood higher on the hill than the windmill's base. The water the windmill pumped up into the tank was carried down to the community by gravity. At the bottom of the windmill was a gasoline engine that could be hooked up when the windy season ended. That was my job when Bill was out at the cow camp.

The first time I looked into the tank, I saw dead rats and birds rotting at the bottom. I asked around and learned that when the water level in the tank got too low, this rotten stuff came through the faucets into the Apaches' homes, causing severe medical problems such as amebic dysentery and trench mouth. It happened to me. After I had been a resident for a while, I had to have all my upper teeth pulled—and I was only twenty-two years old. I suffered intestinal problems that caused me incredible abdominal pain so severe it has remained clear in my memory across nearly fifty years. These stomach disorders happened before I had ever looked into the tank to see what was floating in the water. I initially assumed my ailment was an attack of the flu, but the symptoms came and went for a couple of weeks, and then grew considerably worse. A doctor in Ruidoso diagnosed the condition as amebic dysentery and prescribed sulfa, the miracle drug of the day. He probably saved my life.

When I was physically able, I discussed the filthy and medically hazardous water situation with the authorities at the Mescalero Apache agency at the base of the mountain. They gave me little bottles in which to place samples of the water. As directed, I sent these specimens to the health department in preaddressed mailing tubes. The reports always came back "safe to drink." I knew the water was not safe. A friend took a sample and sent it to a nongovernment laboratory, and that report told a much different story. It read "dangerous for human consumption," and showed high concentrations of coliform bacteria and many other contaminants—animal, vegetable, and mineral. When I told Lonnie Hardin, my supervisor, about the conflicting reports, he was very disturbed and chided me for allowing independent tests to be conducted. He warned me not to tell anyone in the federal service, lest it get back to the agency hierarchy and affect my job. After this personal experience, I began to understand the Apaches' frustration with the bureaucracy and low opinion of anything the government did.

The water at Whitetail was good for washing and for watering a garden, though. The previous teacher had planted a garden, and the vegetable plants loved the water, bacteria and all. Our cabbages were so big that they could barely fit in each side of an orange crate, and the beets had to be cut in quarters and cooked one portion at a time. When I cleaned up after a meal, I would fling the excess contents of a frying pan—grease or whatever else was left—out the back door into the huge hollyhocks that grew right alongside the concrete steps. In the evenings, as soon as I jettisoned the leftovers, I could hear the rush of paws on gravel, and sometimes even a cry of pain if whatever small animal was out there in the dark slurped up the grease before it had sufficiently cooled. I never discovered what type of wildlife enjoyed the hollyhocks, but whatever it was completely consumed the plants.

Surrounding the school property, a fence of barbed wire nailed to rough posts was supposed to prevent invasions by larger animals. Every now and then, however, one outsmarted the barriers and made its way inside, close to our house. Barbed wire was the favorite fencing material at

Whitetail, and miles and miles of it had been strung throughout the community. Much of it still remains, either rolling across now-empty fields or still hanging, rusted, on fence posts.

Usually the barbed wire was up to its task, but I remember that once a little calf slipped inside the compound through a hole in the fence. We tried to feed it, but it refused all our offers. Then we tried to intimidate the poor, scared thing to make it move, but those big brown eyes just looked back at us. One of the Indian cowboys who dropped by simply picked the calf up in his arms like a baby and carried it, mooing and bawling, outside the yard—just like in the movies. The calf had probably learned by example, for the Chiricahuas' fat cows were brazen beasts. They would come right up to a parked car and stick their big heads in the windows as if they owned the place. They did.

The livestock had a history of life at Whitetail beginning long before I got there. In 1913 a majority of the newly released Chiricahua Apache prisoners of war moved from Fort Sill, Oklahoma, to the Mescalero Apache Reservation. During their thirty-year confinement in Florida, Alabama, and Oklahoma, the men had learned how to run cows, and they loved the work. With money earned from the sale of their livestock before release from captivity they purchased cows in New Mexico and began to create their own herd, independent of army or any other supervision. The herd's growth and profitability testified to the skill of the Apache cowboys at Whitetail and to the success of their breeding programs. Their skill was not mine, however, and I have to laugh when I recall the antics of the livestock and my own early incompetence in a rural setting.

Free-roaming bears also lived at Whitetail, and I was completely in terror of them, regardless of their size, cubs included. The Chiricahuas have the right idea. Their cultural customs are quite explicit about bears: they are to be avoided at all costs.[1] The people did this quite well, but of course it failed to keep the bears from wandering around and approaching any place that had food. Every so often I heard a racket fifteen feet or so away from the house, among the old green oil drums where we stored and then burned our trash. For some reason, the drums had no lids. On one particularly black, moonless night, a cacophony of crashing, rattling, and scratching noises arose in the yard.

Trying to appear brave to calm my nervous wife, I leaned out the door and, holding the flashlight as a weapon in my cold and clammy hand, beamed light on the barrels. Two glowing red eyes stared back at me. Suddenly, out jumped a bear—a fuzzy little bear. Scrambling down the side of one of the barrels, he waddled away, most annoyed at my intrusion into his dinner hour.

There were other, more ominous scavengers as well. On a foray along the back roads in the school's pickup truck, I might pass a dead animal surrounded by vultures. These black, ugly, immense birds stood almost a yard tall, their wrinkled red necks extending from humped backs. They probed into the remains of a cadaver and tugged out the entrails, relishing every gulp. Hideous looking as they were, they served an important purpose in nature's plan. They were the rural garbage collectors of the West, and their activities kept flies and disease from spreading. Not incidentally, the vultures also kept the roads clear.

About a year after we arrived at Whitetail, my father-in-law suggested that we buy his car and make monthly payments to him. Our prospects quickly brightened. His vehicle was a sleek, black Chrysler Windsor with something called "Fluid Drive," and it had been maintained so carefully that it got twenty-seven miles to the gallon, an unheard of amount in those days. The only problem was that my wife did not know how to drive—not on smooth highways, and certainly not in mountainous terrain. It was a skill she needed to learn. In case of emergency she would then be able to get medical attention for me or pick me up when the reservation's old pickup had problems. Then, too, if she knew how to drive, she could go for supplies by herself, when I had no time to go along. Basic security in an unfamiliar environment required that both of us be able to drive, especially with Whitetail's unreliable telephone service. All these facts conspired to ensure that she would take the wheel. And so she did, catching on quickly to the stick shift in the school's pickup.

Not too long after she had her first driving lesson from me, she was tooling around the curves on the gravel road down the mountain toward the town of Ruidoso. I warned her to be careful, that driving on gravel could be tricky. She pooh-poohed the idea, and you can guess the rest. Suddenly the back of the vehicle started to spin as we entered a curve. Doris overcorrected and sent the tail in the other direction. The car skidded into a ditch, and there we were, very lucky to land right side up and not on the side of the road with the sheer drop. Shaking, she asked me to take the wheel, but I refused and she finished the drive, albeit at a much slower pace. After cutting her teeth on the old school pickup, driving our new Chrysler dreamboat was a lark. She often drove the car to town.

Although we had no friends there at first, the people in town knew who we were and what we were doing high up on that mountain with the Chiricahua Apaches. They asked many questions about the Indians, who were themselves extremely cautious during their infrequent contacts with the townspeople in both Alamogordo to the south and Ruidoso to the north. And rightfully so, for the Apaches' prior experiences had taught them to be wary of outsiders.

I understand completely now, but I must admit that when I first arrived at Whitetail I was totally unaware of the disasters that had devastated my neighbors. My familiarity with the Chiricahua Apaches was limited to the Hollywood versions of the lives of Geronimo and Cochise. True, the names of Victorio and Mangas Coloradas caused a flicker of recognition as well, but all the rest of the Apaches and their sad history of relations with the American government were a mystery to me.[2]

As we Whitetail residents became more trusting of each other and began to talk, I was surprised to learn that there were other equally important leaders, among them Lozen, Naiche, Nana, Loco, Daklugie, Kanseah, and Chihuahua. These great men and women, not so well known outside the Chiricahua culture, were as important to my neighbors as American presidents are to "white eyes," the Apache nickname for white people. The people's respect for these individuals made me realize that accidents of war often are responsible for forming our lists of heroes and villains and determining our perspective. I quickly saw that Chiricahuas had every right to hate "white eyes." Their treatment at the hands of the U.S. government was so despicable that Dee Brown, author of *Bury My Heart at Wounded Knee* and other popular books, has compared it with the Holocaust in Europe.[3] And there I was, teaching their children the ways of white culture. If I had known the truth about the Chiricahuas' experience with the United States government then, I might have feared, in my ignorance, that they would retaliate against me. But these kindly and charitable survivors never gave me a moment's concern. Had the situation been reversed, I am not certain I would have been as generous and kind.

My neighbor Asa Daklugie, for example, endured almost thirty years of imprisonment in Florida, Alabama, and Oklahoma, during which half of his people died of tuberculosis, smallpox, and other contagious diseases. Son of Nedni Apache Chief Juh, Asa emerged as a leader of those who chose to live at Whitetail when the Chiricahuas were finally released in 1913. When I met Asa for the first time, his face was a mask. He neither smiled nor scowled. He just stared at me for what seemed to be like an embarrassingly long time. Then he simply said, "Hello, teacher." Immediately, without a handshake, he walked on.

Charlie Istee was much more friendly. Charlie would sit on my door step at the teacherage and spin tales of the Indian wars he had participated in under his father's leadership. I was always amazed at his memory for details. Charlie's descriptions opened up an entirely new vista of American history. After all, how many people heard, first hand, about the Apache wars from the Apache side?[4]

Charlie was obviously very proud of his lineage and cultural heritage. Occasionally during those conversations on my steps, I sensed that he was talking to himself, and that, for him, my presence was not important. He seemed to be looking past me or through me to some bygone day. Oh, how I wish I had run inside the teacherage, grabbed a pad and pencil, and taken notes. Of course, if I had done that, it almost certainly would have deterred him from being completely candid with me and from sharing secrets known to few non-Apaches.

The Chiricahuas who visited my home sat for long periods outside on the porch or on the steps, but they never came inside. At the time I did not know that many of the traditional people would never enter an unblessed home, particularly the home of a non-Apache. Whenever I invited them inside, they politely refused. So I sat outside with them, often silently, not understanding, waiting for them to talk. I was a very willing listener, but in truth, I was overcome by the fact that here were the sons and daughters of the great Apache nation. I hesitated to offend anyone through my ignorance of their cultural customs, so I never spoke out of turn, I tried not to say the wrong thing, and I resisted the impulse to ask foolish questions. I appreciated the silence and mistakenly interpreted it as my visitors' reticence to share tribal confidences. However, I eventually learned it was more a cultural pause, a time to collect long-gone spirits. While there actually was a reluctance among the Chiricahuas to talk about themselves, they liked to talk about their experiences.

During those peaceful pauses I observed and enjoyed the natural environment surrounding Whitetail. I suppose I had expected New Mexico to be full of palm trees and hot sand, like Tempe. Whitetail was quite a surprise. The silence there could be profound. Sometimes the whooshing of birds' wings was the only sound. Brightly colored birds flew around the house in the summer, filling the air with red, green, blue, and yellow. Across the way, I watched the dashing and darting roadrunners with fascination. I loved their comical gait as they goose-stepped frenziedly back and forth across the dirt road, avoiding cars or whatever they imagined the danger to be. Hawks and eagles circled above and sometimes perched atop the tall pines, razor talons clutching the swaying branches while sharp eyes spied on us and kept watch when we least knew it.

Photography was my hobby, and I tried very hard to capture this wildlife and other scenes of interest on film. Occasionally I was successful, and then I hurried to my darkroom in the teacherage basement to process the film. My Federal Enlarger handled both 35 mm film and also the 120 mm film that my Ansco Automatic Reflex used. The hardest part of the process was developing the negatives. An egg timer ticked away while I see-sawed the film back and forth in a tray of developer, the method we used in the days before developing tanks. Often I felt my muscles turn to knots before the little bell rang. Time seemed to go so slowly in the total dark, but I hesitated to risk using the safe light. When I was processing the prints, I used a small yellow-orange safe light that gave the room a warm and friendly glow. I could see the images emerging from the paper as it floated in the developer. There was no plumbing in the darkroom, so I had to tote everything upstairs to wash, or bring the water down. I seldom objected to doing all this to produce a print or two.

Almost everything at Whitetail was pleasant, give or take. For example, summertime was not very hot during the day, and it was cool most nights, promoting a sound, refreshing sleep that was especially welcome after a long evening spent in the basement processing film. In the mornings, the sun warmed up the air fairly quickly, and I learned one curious fact about mountain air: a person can roast in the sun and freeze in the deep shade. Winters at that high altitude were deceiving. With the mercury hovering not far above zero, a hearty individual could feel comfortable without a coat for a while ... unless the wind blew. But an intelligent person would not tempt fate.

I learned from practical experience that freezing comes sooner than expected and that frostbite happens without warning. A load of wash hanging on the line one day during our first winter at Whitetail froze solid. I carried in flat shirts with the arms outstretched and pajama bottoms that looked as if they were cut from cardboard. I could hardly get them in the door. The arm of one shirt broke off when it hit the door frame, creating a sleeveless summer shirt.

At any time of the year the night sky at Whitetail twinkled with a crowded canopy of stars. The thin air at that altitude was so pure and clean that nothing got between an observer and the universe. I began to understand why the ancients attributed deity to the constellations in the days before humankind's architecture and pollution problems obstructed the celestial view.

We always welcomed the gentle, warm mountain rains that fell frequently throughout all the seasons except winter. Some tribes call these the "female" rains in contrast to more violent thunderstorms, which are known as "male" rains, but the Chiricahuas made no such distinction. Many times I looked up through the tall pines and watched high-pressure ridges build up into giant cumulus clouds that erupted into unforgettable sound and fury. I could watch the birth of cloud babies, which remained nearly invisible until they reached dew point at seven to nine thousand feet. New fluffs of woolly white would form there and join the congregating flock. As they were pushed higher and higher, they merged to form the huge monsters that exploded in deafening blasts that shook the ground, rattled the windows, and caused my masonry house to shudder on its foundations. Then, huddled together with the dogs and cats, trembling, we would watch as all around us the wild animals headed for shelter under the spreading branches of hospitable trees.

The Apaches helped me learn how to judge how soon the storm would reach us. Count out the seconds between the flashes of lightning and the boom, multiply by one thousand, and then you have an estimate in miles of the distance to the deluge. While not exactly correct, it was a piece of their folklore that I cherished. When a storm hit, water would rush down the dirt road and fill the ditch alongside it. Torrential rains occasionally wiped out the road altogether, and sometimes we were completely cut off from the rest of the reservation and from the town of Ruidoso. I remember seeing a twenty-foot-deep canyon west of Mescalero that had been gouged out in one flash flood.

During these boomers, normal conversation naturally had to pause, and we would wait under the porch roof in silence for the half an hour or so that it usually took for the convulsion to pass. Then the sun would come out and light up the droplets of rainwater clinging to the tips of pine needles and blades of wild grasses. Talking would resume, usually about the storm. The freshly cleaned air always carried a heavenly fragrance of pine and cedar as a farewell gift, at least for a couple of hours, until the trees and ground dried.

Another new delight for me at Whitetail was our pets. As a young child, I was extremely allergic to cats and dogs and could survive in a house with them for only about fifteen minutes before I began scratching, coughing, and then wheezing. At Whitetail I had a place where I could keep my pets outdoors, and it was wonderful to have the joy of dogs and cats without the consequences.

My first animal pal when I lived among the Apaches was a cat about a year old. Then came a yellow kitten, just weaned. Next, one of the students offered me a puppy which resulted from an amorous affair between his bitch and a local coyote. I named him Jiggs after the comic strip character "Jiggs and Maggie," since the big cat was named Maggie. These three comprised the main body of a continuous stream of animal residents for two years.

Jiggs was gone for a few days once and came home with a couple of pups. He was very proud of his charges and took his duties seriously. The pups eventually found other homes when they grew to be self-supporting.

When the weather turned cold, Maggie and the little yellow kitten would sneak into the school's kitchen and hide in cozy warmth in back of the big black oven. One day Dorcie, the cook, complained that my cat had "baked a cake" under the oven. I had to clean it up. The little guy often came into the schoolroom when warmer weather allowed me to prop open the doors and windows. He (or she, as it may have been) jumped up on my desk and batted my pen as I tried to write. The children were supposed to be facing front and working hard on their assignments, but I heard ripples of laughter around the room. Sometimes the cat marched up and down the aisles and played with tiny balls of paper dropped accidentally or on purpose by the kids. He was a real entertainer and frequently broke up the classroom boredom.

Gentle Jiggs also liked to play with the children, but he had one major fault: he loved to chase cars. He would stand back from the dirt road until a car gained momentum and then dash madly after it, always too close for comfort. One day a car drove over his snout. He was a pitiful sight; his nose was literally bent out of shape. Jiggs moped around until school was out and then I took him to a veterinarian in Ruidoso. The doctor wired his head and told me to feed him only liquids for a while. When I brought him back home, he lounged dejectedly atop his house. To my great surprise, the cat Maggie cuddled up next to him and licked his wounds. I learned something about animal psychology from these two, believe me.

One rainy day a truck driver knocked on my door and apologetically informed me that he had driven over my dog. The ground was wet and soggy, but I trudged out to the scene of the purported tragedy to reclaim my pet. I found a dog-shaped mold in the mud, but there was no dog in it. The next morning a forlorn-looking beast staggered to my back door. A week later Jiggs was good as new. Too bad he learned nothing from that experience. When I left Whitetail, I willed the dog to the students, but a logging truck finally did him in.

In autumn the Chiricahuas bundled up and continued to visit me on my porch, talking softly in their way, with words as gentle as a female rain. They never imposed themselves and often never even let me know they were in the vicinity of the teacherage. Every cold morning, whether or not anyone was expected on the porch, I would bring my clothes from the bedroom closet and lay them on a chair in the living room next to the heater grate. I would stand on the grate, hurriedly pulling on underwear as I soaked up the warmth radiating from the floor. In a few seconds my stockinged feet would become uncomfortably hot. In the meantime, my clothes were warming on the chair. As soon as I slipped on my trousers, I had to hurry to get into my shoes to keep from scorching my socks. For such a small heating system, it did an amazingly efficient job in keeping the house comfortably warm.

Outside, the crisp fall breeze routinely stayed all day, often coming inside on a sunny afternoon through an open window and shuffling my papers or blowing them across the room. The wind, regardless of how strong or weak it was, always lifted the ever-present dust from the road to everyone's mouth and eyes and made little dunes on the windowsills. At night when the wind stopped, the silence was awesome. Even the coyotes at Whitetail stopped howling during these periods of stillness; perhaps they were listening to human conversations, which could be heard more than a quarter of a mile away. As I adapted more and more to the environment, I found myself speaking in hushed tones to my visitors and my wife, as if I were in a great cathedral. I was.

The sunrises and sunsets on the mountain were spectacular, and I tried hard to capture them on film. Usually a light scattering of clouds first reflected a brilliant gold, then became tinged with soft rose and carmine. Burgundy followed, and at last a rich purple melted into violet and blueblack. Then it was dark. The most dazzling displays occurred when a thick blanket of stratus clouds left just enough room for fingers of the sun to peek through before it snuggled under for the night. Then the sky would blaze with subtly shifting shades and hues. I never knew when to trip my shutter because of the constantly changing panorama.

After darkness arrived, it seemed that the forest went to sleep and peace filled the air. It sank deep into my bones, and I felt at one with nature and God. On these occasions, I recalled that the Biblical prophets looked for God in the mountains. At Whitetail, I could understand why.

Chapter 2
The Whitetail Day School

The school at Whitetail was surrounded by small farms tended by former Chiricahua Apache prisoners of war, their relatives, and their children. A gravel thoroughfare just wide enough for two cars ran through the village, and many unpaved, rutted trails wandered over hills and across streams, meandering past the government-constructed homes secluded within the forest.

There were two school buses, a little orange one and, after it died, its green successor. Only six to eight children could comfortably fit inside these vehicles. Often the kids were crammed in so tightly that some had to hang out the windows. They did not mind in the least, and they had a great time waving their arms from the bus windows and stretching toward the road.

Covering the fifteen- to twenty-mile (one way) bus route took about forty-five minutes each day. Usually the bus was driven by an Apache driver, but occasionally I drove it. The first morning route started about eight o'clock and took the bus toward the "summit," the highest spot on the main road running through the middle of the community. Many log cabins perched alongside the main thoroughfare. Because there were no hutches to shelter the waiting children, in bad weather the Apache kids stayed indoors until the bus arrived, then waded through sucking mud to get to the road. They would clamber up into the vehicle, cowboy boots and galoshes flopping and oozing. These kids, however, were the more fortunate ones.

Some of the students who lived in the other direction came from homes beside the road, but others lived deep in the forest, and they also had to be picked up by the bus. The "roads" to their houses were often little more than ruts carved at crazy angles on a hillside. Nonetheless, the little yellow (or green) school bus chugged and bumped and rolled from side to side toward their houses as well, except when the byways became totally impassable due to inclement weather. Then the children had to walk out to a more accessible location. The bus often seemed about to capsize as it navigated in and out of the trees and up and down the high and low sides of mud holes as the kids hooted, yelled, and bounced on the seats.

Rain or shine, if a student did not appear at the bus stop, I found out why. Eugene Chihuahua's grandchildren lived the farthest from the school in a really remote spot of the back country, and, understandably, every now and then they would miss a day of lessons. If the excuses other students muttered for their friends' absences sounded implausible, I made a personal visit to the family. When the weather turned stormy, some Apache kids stayed overnight with relatives who lived nearer the school.

The bus was housed in the school's garage, one part of the "complex," so to speak, of buildings. The complex also included two "teacherages," or homes for teachers. Doris and I occupied one house; the other was vacant, probably constructed in bygone days when there were sufficient pupils to require two teachers at Whitetail.

A beautiful hand-carved and painted sign identified the school, but the Indian represented on it wore a full-feathered headdress, typical of those worn by the Northern Plains Indians. As I grew more and more aware of Native American history, the sign became a symbol to me—it was one more piece of evidence that our government lumped all Indians together regardless of tribe. Ironically, the sign was not even necessary. Anyone really familiar with Indian education could not mistake the buildings for anything other than U.S. property. They were yellow-stuccoed and green-trimmed, as were most other government schools everywhere in the country. However, we had something at Whitetail that not too many other schools had: a cattle guard, still omnipresent in the ranchlands of the West.

This structure marked the entry to the school compound and was made out of old train rails laid about six inches apart for about six feet over a pit in the ground. The cattle guard was ten to fifteen feet wide and was specifically designed to keep livestock out of the yard. Sometimes it worked and sometimes it didn't. Cattle and horses never liked to traverse the rails. They risked breaking a leg by slipping into the spaces between, and somehow they knew it. A little gate and a path alongside the cattle guard enabled a horse and rider to bypass the rails and enter. If a rider felt particularly adventuresome, he and his mount could leap up and over into the school yard, but most folks avoided the risk.

I had been given a partial list of prospective pupils and was expected to determine who had moved away and who might have moved in, and which Chiricahua children had reached kindergarten age in the last year. Kids came and went. They would come to visit Grandma and Grandpa or Auntie and Uncle for a school year and then move back to their parents' house, wherever that was.

My wife and I arrived at Whitetail about a week before school was to begin. I had only that much time to get everything ready for my pupils, which caused butterflies and panic in my innards. I had to prepare lesson plans for six grades plus kindergarten for every day and I had no past teaching experience to help me. I remember walking around my empty classroom in the lonely stillness, locating pencils, paper, test books, chalk, and all the necessary items that make up a schoolroom. I can still hear the hollow echo of my steps on the wooden floors of that room. I wrote my name on the blackboard which stretched the entire length of the wall opposite my rickety desk.

I was responsible not only for the kids but also for all the property within the school's three- or four-acre compound. When I finished reconnoitering my vacant school, I creaked back in my desk chair and said a silent prayer that I would be worthy of everyone's faith in me. I really wanted to be a good teacher and community leader (my own wish, not a BIA requirement), and the weight of that responsibility destroyed any residual peace I had maintained since arriving at Whitetail.

Back outside and breathing the delicious mountain air, I took notice of the dense weeds around the school yard. Two sets of wooden stairs on the sides of the building led to the two classrooms; one was in a sad state of disrepair but the weeds loved it. They had climbed up the handrail.

A bit scared and somewhat worried, I went back to our silent house. No radio, no phonograph broke the stillness; television, of course, was a still a thing of the future. There were only a few books and some art supplies to pass the long evening hours and quiet my mounting anxiety. It is not surprising that one of our first purchases after my check arrived was a tabletop Arvin radio-phonograph. At our high altitude we could pick up a number of stations, some as far away as Texas, too many of them evangelists begging for money.

The next morning I heard bustling and shuffling in the schoolyard next door. When I looked out, I saw an Indian man pumping gas into the school's green pickup. I crunched across the gravel to greet and meet Levi Hosetosewit, the bus driver and school custodian. In awkward conversation (at least on my part), he said he was also new at the job. Levi was a Comanche whose mother had married Eugene Chihuahua, one of Whitetail's leaders. When she divorced him and left Whitetail, Levi decided to remain. He was a good ice breaker and had no trouble communicating, despite his (to me) bizarre grammar and pronunciation. In the spirit of friendship, I invited him into the teacherage for a soda, but he was reluctant. Later, this reticence to enter my home seemed to be the norm at Whitetail, perhaps because of the traditional customs; only a few brave souls made it past the door.

In typical bureaucratic fashion, the government sent out an official to conduct an inventory of the school's supplies and furnishings and obtain my signature verifying their presence, but he was delayed for a few weeks. Before he made his way to Whitetail, I discovered a tremendous fire hazard in the school's attic. There were piles of broken chairs and greasy old pillows that we were not allowed to destroy because they were still on the government's register. Not having signed for them yet, I took these nasty articles outside and burned them. I also pulled down an old, totally useless shed that was a danger to the kids. When the government agent at long last arrived, I insisted on a new inventory. He compared the property with the old list, and simply wrote "wind storm" to explain the missing shed, and "mysterious disappearance" to account for the rest, to my great relief.

In the school's basement were a refectory and a first-aid station equipped to handle all minor medical emergencies from bug bites to broken legs. Being an emergency medical technician was also part of my job because the public health doctors assigned to the reservation would not make calls at Whitetail. In the two years I lived among the Chiricahuas and taught their children, not one physician that I knew of visited the community, although a dentist appeared every now and then. As I recall, he was a shabbily dressed fellow who wore worn slacks and a loud flowered shirt and carried what looked like a mechanic's tool box. On his first visit he introduced himself as the government dentist and, using the smaller classroom as his "office," he called the kids in one at a time. He did no drilling or filling. He simply pulled the children's teeth, without any anesthetic, and then offered his services to me. I respectfully declined. To his credit the dentist examined all the kids before he left—spare none.

The school had a neat split of a dozen boys and a dozen girls. Each row in both classrooms, a larger one and a smaller one, had a different grade, from kindergarten to sixth, again fairly evenly divided as to gender and grade. The seventh and eighth grades had been dropped; students in that age group were sent away to the Indian School in Albuquerque, about two hundred miles north, if they elected to go. Unlike the prisoner-of-war children sixty-odd years earlier—the ancestors of my pupils—these kids were given a choice. When they left Whitetail, they sent messages to their folks any way they could, just like most kids away from home, but at Whitetail, unlike many home bases, telephones were at a premium.

The teacherage had one of the only two telephones in the entire community. It was an antiquated wooden box contraption with a crank on the side and, below the mouthpiece, a small slanted surface that was perfect for jotting notes. Besides a general emergency ring that everyone knew, one long ring followed by a short one brought the Mescalero operator on the line. I could then be connected with any agency number I wished. Going through the switchboard was unnecessary if the party being called was on the same line and the caller knew the correct ring. If the switchboard worker was on coffee break, anyone else on the reservation-wide system might pick up the telephone out of curiosity or because they had mistaken that ring for theirs. People did pick up randomly, causing the line voltage to drop, but no one seemed to mind the lack of privacy. All of us were thankful just to have such utilities. It could have been worse, and had been, not too long before my wife and I arrived.

Rural electric power had just been brought to Whitetail, and the lines were still loosely draped on rough wooden poles alongside the road down the entire seventeen miles to the highway. Before that, the only source of electricity was a gas-driven generator housed near the garage within the school compound. When wind or other weather knocked out the juice, the faithful generator was drafted into service again, huffing and puffing until the power was restored. Power outages at Whitetail sometimes lasted for several days, so every home kept handy a kerosene lamp, candles, matches, and flashlights for emergencies.

The school at Whitetail was more than just an educational institution. It was the focal point of activity for the entire Chiricahua Apache community. In addition to the dispensary and the telephone, the school complex had the only gas pump, and there was a public water tap anyone could use when their own pipes froze or broke. Few homes had insulated pipes, and most Apaches drained their lines before every freeze to keep them from breaking.

Dances, socials, public meetings, and movies were also held at the school. Every week or so we would have a regular movie for everyone, reels of film straight from Hollywood, brought from town along with a big old black-enameled Holmes Educator. The Holmes was an antique 35 mm machine with gold scrolling gracing the edges. I was made to understand by my supervisors that the government could not afford a new 16 mm projector for the Apaches (almost all public schools had one), so the Holmes, born long before 16 mm was even invented, had to do. It was an unwieldy creature and often broke the film, which I repaired. During those first-aid treatments, and during reel changes, I sold candy and soda pop at outrageous prices. The extra money was used to buy tools and machinery for the village. It was the only way we could replenish what we needed for communal use.

When I showed a western, it was an eye-opener to hear the audience, kids and adults alike, cheer for the Indians and boo the cavalry. Knowing that the people around me were the losers in their war against the United States occasionally gave me an uncomfortable feeling, especially during these movies. But as I grew more and more familiar with the Chiricahuas, I developed grave misgivings about who was right and who was wrong in America's relations with Indian tribes. Those questions remain today.

Each time a memory surfaces or something I see or hear jogs my mind, I recall even more about those years teaching the Chiricahua children. Modern school holidays, with carefree students swarming in shopping malls, bring to mind the unscheduled days off at Whitetail when we all picked piñon nuts—tiny, delectable morsels that fall from piñon pine cones in the fall. Folk wisdom says that every seven years the trees will be heavy with the nuts, but at Whitetail, the size of each year's crop was fairly unpredictable. When piñon season arrived, there was no use having school because no one would come. So I collected the kids in the school's pickup and drove out to a promising field of pine trees. They could clean out a tree rapidly, filling whole buckets full of the tasty treats. Whether they ate them raw or roasted them first over a fire was a personal choice; the Apaches loved piñons any way they could get them. Most of the kids brought a bag or pocketful to school to munch on during recess or whenever they thought they could get away with it. Now and then I would ask a question during class and find a pupil sitting with eyes bugged out and cheeks stuffed like a squirrel, able to do nothing but grunt. Everyone else laughed but I kept a straight face, at least until I got home.

Other unscheduled holidays also popped up now and then. One day I took the kids up to Pajarito Mountain to the U.S. Forestry Service lookout tower. It was a fairly long drive over rough trails for the old bus and the pickup, but luckily the ground was comparatively level most of the way to the mountain. We started climbing about ten o'clock in the morning, keeping a wary eye on the sky for storms. The road was narrow and switched back and forth. I wondered what I would do if I met someone coming down or if a sudden cloudburst drenched the narrow road and turned it into a quagmire. There would be little warning and no place to go in either case except for the few pull-offs known as "turnarounds" that had been grudgingly carved out of rock over the years. One of us would have to back down or up. My blood ran cold, and still does, imagining what it would be like to go back down that mountain in reverse.

Fortunately, on that trip we had no trouble, and the fantastic view from the top was well worth the trouble getting there. After a chorus of "oohs" and "aahs," the kids and I struggled up many shaky metal steps to the lookout tower and crowded in. The ranger showed us his map with the surveying telescope on top of it and told us how he could triangulate a fire by swiveling it around and coordinating with two other towers that were barely perceptible in the distance. The kids looked eagerly through the scope and had a great deal of trouble getting their eyes unglued to allow the next student to have a turn. We could see almost two hundred miles of scenic beauty in any direction.

The ranger showed us his radio-telephone and told a few stories about his adventures in the tower. One day, he said, a fire came so close that he could feel its heat, and he almost had to evacuate. I found the constant wind annoying. There was a steady gale at that height, and I had to lean into it at a forty-five-degree angle to keep from being blown away. Naturally, it did not bother the kids.

On the way back down the mountain I tried to keep everyone from bailing out or jettisoning fellow classmates from the pickup. We stayed fairly close behind the old orange bus for the first several hundred feet, proceeding very slowly in case someone was coming up from below. As we rounded an outside bend, I noticed that the bus was gaining distance from us too fast. I saw gravel spin off as it took the next turn. Another curve and it was out of sight. My pickup truck's rear end was dancing all over the dirt road's washboard surface, and the kids were bouncing like bronco riders. I was truly scared. Coming down the last incline and out onto a level section, I saw the bus parked with the driver and the kids waiting outside. I was ready to lambaste the poor fellow, but then I saw that he was sweating and shaking. "The brakes gave out up there," he cried, "and I didn't think we were going to make it." I said nothing and led the way slowly back to Whitetail. The kids thought it was a blast, and we talked about it in class for a long time afterward, at least until the next field trip.

The regular school vacation schedule was not observed at Whitetail. Columbus Day, for example, was never even mentioned. How do you tell a class of Apaches whose ancestors have lived in this country for hundreds of years that an Italian sailor discovered their land a few hundred years ago? I also had a problem explaining how the West was won, at least according to the government's point of view, and why the pioneers were not prosecuted for stealing the Indians' land. All these intrusions into my honest misconceptions slowed me down and forced me to think about everything I said before I said it. In the process, I was marked for life.

If the truth about American history was difficult for me to deal with, the language barrier was even worse. Most of my pupils had only a rudimentary command of English, but I was still infected with my ivory tower vernacular and an inflated and sophisticated vocabulary. The first time I spoke in the classroom, dozens of blank, uncomprehending little faces stared back at me, totally oblivious to what I was saying. I had to learn to communicate all over again, and I tried to remember that fact each morning as I stepped out the door to walk the few feet to the school.

I knew I was not a good teacher, and it made me terribly self-conscious in front of the children. My academic training and practice teaching back in southern Illinois had been in secondary education. I knew next to nothing about the primary grades, much less about teaching in a one- or two-room school where I was the only instructor. To make matters worse, the kids I was teaching came from a nonmidwestern, nonwhite background, and I initially found that very disconcerting. The greenest of teachers, I had only a couple of days of meetings with other Indian day school teachers to learn a few tricks. And I had absolutely no personal preparation for the formidable task of living among Native Americans. When I recently started reading nonfiction books written from inside the culture about the Chiricahua Apaches, I was retrospectively amazed that the people put up with me.

Each day, before anyone else arrived in the classroom, I drew vertical lines on the large blackboard that covered the front wall. The lines divided sections for each class from sixth grade down to second grade and enclosed each day's assignments. The kids in those grades could read while I organized the younger children. Still alone in the building, I set up the little side room with toys and projects for the kindergartners and put crayons and paper out for the first graders. When all was in place, I sat at my desk and brooded for a moment, silently praying that I could make it until lunch, or at least until recess. Then I plodded across the gravel to my home to have breakfast and wait for the school bus to arrive.

When the last group of kids emerged from "Old Yellow," our school bus, I would check my watch. Right on the stroke of the hour, I would step outside the door and ring the old hand bell to call the class in. After they had piled into their seats, I would point out the day's lessons to each class as written on the board. The kindergartners were last; I enjoyed reading stories to them because they gave me their undivided attention. Often I wondered if their minds, too, were far away, running through the high grasses at Whitetail, perhaps chasing their dogs or a horse. Mine often was.

My teaching technique varied from day to day. I had no real curriculum. I just passed from subject to subject, row to row, class to class, like a ship sailing along with no final destination. I taught the older students a little about world history, tried small scientific experiments, even told a joke now and then to make a lesson more interesting and digestible. I could never find a clue in all those big innocent eyes as to whether or not anything was soaking in. It was like prying out horseshoe nails to get a response from them. On the other hand, I was always afraid that someone would interrupt with a comment or question, because once I got off the track, I had trouble getting back. I worried that I would lose control of the class before I could build up enough steam to plow through whatever I was teaching. I constantly felt that I was not always reaching everyone. Some were too young to comprehend, others were bored. Was there proof of my shortcoming? The kids practically raced out the door at recess time.

During my first couple of weeks at the school, the children talked in Apache to each other but in English to me. Unlike some of the other schools attended by Indian children, the Chiricahua youngsters were never punished for conversing with each other in their native language. One morning, at the end of one particularly trying week, they decided to test me. Like mischievous kids anywhere, they conspired mightily against the teacher. Looking me right in the eye, they spoke in Apache and then giggled and hooted when I obviously failed to understand. That afternoon I got even. Speaking in German, I gave them their assignments and then sat down. After a while I asked, in English, how they were coming along. One courageous little guy was the spokesperson. He said that nobody had understood me, and I answered, "For not finishing your assignments, you won't have recess today." Their faces fell. Then I added, "But I'll make you a deal. I won't speak in German to you if you don't speak in Apache to me." They understood clearly, and I never had that particular trouble again. Even the school's cook had to chuckle at that one.

Learning their language was never an option for me. Before I ever started teaching my supervisor explained that it would be impossible for me to learn the Apache language because it was not written and was always changing. That sounded odd, but I soon found out what he meant. While it is the nature of languages to be dynamic, the Apache tongue carries the concept to extremes. For example, if there is no word for a particular item or if the person speaking cannot remember an accepted expression, the unwritten rules of the language permit the speaker to simply make one up! To illustrate, someone (it may have been Kanseah, Jr.) told me that there is only one Apache word for "implement." It can mean "knife," "fork," "hoe," "shovel," "pencil," etc. A speaker who wants to be more specific either makes up a new Apache word or uses an English word. As Apache linguistic flexibility enables everyone to have a different name for "knife," for example, I might call it one thing, and you might call it another. If we were discussing the knife, we would have to speak of it as "that implement we use to lift food to our mouths" and hope each understood what the other meant.

Later, I discovered another aspect of the language's complexity and beauty—that the names of the people have specific meanings, such as "rainbow." In keeping with an ancient custom, once the bearer of a name dies, the word that was her name is never used again. When Rainbow passes on, any reference made to her substitutes a circumlocution for her name, something like "that great band of colors which sweeps across the sky."

During my tenure at Whitetail I heard many English words used in Apache conversations. The mixture of languages was sad to me, as I believed that the bilingualism would contribute to the disappearance of the original tongue. But a ray of hope was still present then: the children spoke fluent Apache among themselves and with adults, and it was always a pleasure for me to hear it. I often eavesdropped on conversations between the kids and the bus drivers or the cooks. I never understood a word, but the good feelings came through. Later in life I realized that the generation of children I taught was probably the last group of Chiricahuas to speak the language. These days, English is the preferred tongue on the reservation among the younger Apaches.

One day I reentered the classroom after I had stepped out to see the cook and found that the things on my desk had been moved around. I felt I had to show authority or I would lose the class. Not a soul was looking at me, so I cleared my throat loudly and asked, "Who was at my desk?" I got no response, so I tried again, this time walking up and down the aisles looking at everyone. They all had guilty expressions. Finally I said, "OK, no recess until I find out." (Taking recess away was the greatest punishment I could mete out.) One fellow sitting in the rear of the room, where no one but me could see him, pointed wordlessly toward the other side of the room—the kindergarten and first grade section. Over there, one little boy was hiding his head. I paused at each desk until I reached his, then looked back over at the accuser. He nodded. I took the small boy's head in my hands and asked, "Did you touch anything on my desk?" A small tear trickled down his expressionless face, and he gave an almost imperceptible nod of assent. I dismissed everyone else and then had a heart-to-heart chat with him, explaining why it was important not to go through my things, or anyone else's, without their permission. Quietly and gently, I said, "From now on, if I find anything missing, I'll think of you." He shook his head from side to side, letting me know that he did not want that to happen. I asked him what he wanted from my desk, and he pointed to an eraser. His own had broken off his pencil. After that, I put a soup can with pencils in it on my desk, free for the taking. So much for being a stern disciplinarian.

I cannot recall an open rebellion against me, although the kids were capable of that. If they did anything wrong, it was when I looked away. Shortly after the "eraser caper," one older fellow passed my desk to go to his seat. He deliberately reached over and moved my pen holder. After he did it, he turned to me and grinned from ear to ear. I only waved my finger at him, and smiled back.

One of the girls in the upper grades tried my patience severely by her actions. She seemed to be a lightning rod for trouble; bad things just happened around her. As she left the school's kitchen–dining room after lunch one day, she spat in the sink. Our cook caught her and made her clean it up, telling her that no one should spit in the sink because dishes were washed there. Angry because she had to clean the sink, she pouted the rest of the day. The next day, she and a few friends refused to come to school. Finally, her grandfather, Jasper Kanseah, Sr., a respected elder, came to the school to find out what was wrong. The girl had been telling a very different story at home, saying that she had found a hair in her food and she would never eat at that school again. When Grandpa learned the truth, he got after the girls and they showed up the next day. If she did not know it already, I guess she learned that day that her grandfather (and others among the older Chiricahuas) could not be fooled. Happily, this particular difficult student grew up to be a very fine woman and had a child of her own.

The subject of history, one of my favorites, seemed to have no grade demarcations, and so I held many lectures for the entire school on the topic. I used my theatrical bent to make history interesting, but I got the feeling from the kids that only the present mattered to them. My mind was always racing for ways to make figures and places come alive, but I was painfully aware that the kids' experiences didn't reach much beyond Whitetail. It angered me that the schoolbooks I had to use took such a negative view of Indians. I knew that the children were learning their heritage at home, but it should have been taught in classrooms as well, to demonstrate that this nation of many cultures valued each one. I came to believe that the kids had a right to hear their history and culture presented side by side with the European history and culture.

After all, these Apache children were just like other students—and like other children, for that matter. Each child had a unique personality. Some were always quiet and shy, some were mischievous and rowdy. Some were polite and eager to please. Some were beginning to be curious about the differences between them and white people. And some appeared just completely bored by everything about school. I saw a transformation as soon as they cleared the door at the end of the school day. Their eyes began to glow. They shouted with exuberance. They jumped and ran and pushed and pulled. It was like freeing convicts from their cells. I felt sad that the things I said held little interest, that there was a great wall separating us. Sure, they were friendly to me away from the classroom, and sometimes even warm and eager, but my role as a teacher placed a barrier between us that I did not dare to drop. And that was too bad, because I lost a lot in the process.

Through all of these experiences, I always had the support of the school's cook, Dorcie Kazhe, who had replaced Delores Enjady. She was from the Pima-Papago tribe, but had married an Apache and lived with her family at Whitetail. She was picked up each day by the bus driver. As soon as she reached the school, she went down the concrete steps to the basement to begin preparing the noon meal. Actually, she did more than just cook. She dusted the kids with DDT for head lice, made certain they showered at least once a week, applied minor first aid, and cleaned the kitchen and the infirmary areas. The bus driver also had other responsibilities. He was the school's custodian, with duties that included cleaning the upstairs classrooms and lavatories. He kept the walks cleaned and swept, and hacked away the thick wild vegetation in the fall to keep it from climbing the stairs into the classrooms, and kept the gas pump and outbuildings free from all the underbrush. The yard constantly needed care, and there were always many repairs that had to be made.

I discovered early on that most of the Apaches at Whitetail were self-reliant, creative, and patient people. In that isolated area everyone had to be handy at a number of things; getting into town for repairs was not easy. When a problem had everyone stumped, which was seldom, they would look at a damaged piece of equipment, for example, shake their heads, and lament, "Isn't that awful?" Then I knew all hope was lost, temporarily at least.

One of our bus drivers doubled as a carpenter when the kids put on a Christmas program at school for their parents and grandparents. He built a crib for the baby Jesus and found wood to make shepherds' staffs. He and I built the stage by binding classroom benches together. On the platform we propped some tall, tattered old window screens. For background we used poster paint on butcher paper, kindly donated down the mountain by the tribal store's proprietor. We tacked the scenery onto the screens and lashed them together. Our cook and some of the students' mothers made costumes out of old sheets and dyed them with vegetal colors supplied by plants growing in the Whitetail earth. My photographic reflectors completed the dramatic effect, and the religious program was a huge success.[1]

No doubt many memories reawakened in the Whitetail audience on the night of our Christmas pageant, and some new ones were made as well. In particular, having noticed a need for a special type of receptacle during past group gatherings, in advance of the Christmas program I asked the kids to bring empty cans from home. Excitedly, they decorated the tin containers and wrapped them carefully. When the Christmas program was over, the polite Apaches voiced their thanks, not only for the program but also for the useful and considerate personal touch: spittoons.

Chapter 3
IF Only I Had Known . . .

Looking at the Chiricahua kids every school day (and on weekends), I saw faces that naturally resembled those of their grandparents, the mighty Chiricahua Apaches. During the time of the frontier West, the Chiricahuas, my neighbors and friends, had been among the most feared people in America. Certainly, successive generations of Americans have read or heard about Geronimo and his escapades across the Southwest. A hundred years ago these children would have been considered enemies of the United States and Mexico. They would have been fair game, hated and hunted by the armies and people of two nations.

The Chiricahuas' reputation for ferocity, earned over years of bloody resistance to Mexican and American government policies, grew until finally it became impossible to separate myth from reality. While the kids' bloodlines could not be denied, the whole scenario disturbed and confused me.

For one thing, it was hard for me to believe that Mrs. Coonie, the tiny old woman who fed and cared for a large number of stray dogs, had been the Apache warrior Dahteste. Chiricahua Apache oral tradition records that this gentle woman, whom I often saw riding her burro along the dirt road, was as courageous, daring, and skillful in battle as any Apache man. It was easy to figure out what *that* meant. She and Lozen, another warrior, were the women in whom Geronimo had such faith that he sent them to negotiate early surrender terms with the U.S. Army.

Contemporary Chiricahua Apache woman Elbys Hugar, the great-granddaughter of Cochise, once lived at Whitetail with her family. She remembered Mrs. Coonie from those days: "Dahteste was always dressed nicely in her Apache clothing. She wore beautiful beads, turquoise sometimes, and a very pretty belt. I always admired her beaded bags. She wore her hair straight. Just brushed it out. I don't think I ever saw her braid her hair. She was a nice-looking woman, very nice looking. Dahteste owned a lot of sheep and hired a Mexican man as sheepherder.... She was a Christian woman and went to the [Dutch] Reformed Church at Whitetail."[1]

When I first saw Dahteste, she was nearly one hundred years old, but she had never lost her fire. She spent hours sitting on her porch talking with Apache visitors about the days before the white man arrived in Apache country. To her last day on earth she refused to speak English, but somehow she felt no conflict in attending Sunday church services.

Today, Dahteste's house at Whitetail has collapsed inward, and only one wall stands precariously to mark the spot where so much history lived. Barbed wire lies everywhere on her land, tangled on the ground or dangling from tree stumps used as fence posts. To the rear, the lush overgrown land slopes upward for a little more than a hundred yards until the incline ends atop a ridge. There sits the Istee house and barn, once home to my friend Charlie and his family, descendants of the famous Chief Victorio of the Warm Springs Apache group.

Jasper Kanseah, Jr., who as a lad of thirteen had been taken prisoner along with his Uncle Geronimo and other members of Geronimo's band, was an elder at Whitetail. He had been a horse holder for and apprentice to the Chiricahua warrior Yah-no-sha. Had the surrender not occurred, the adult Jasper Kanseah would have become a fierce fighter for the Apache way. When I knew him, he was a soft-spoken older gentleman with many grandchildren. Long before I arrived, he had been a policeman on the Mescalero Apache Reservation. He was also, along with Dahteste and many other Chiricahuas, a member in good standing of the Dutch Reformed Church.

How could these and the many other Chiricahua Apache adults I lived among at Whitetail have been such cruel and evil enemies of the United States? I saw a gentle people, hardworking, respectful, and smiling, and enriched by a spirituality I could not, at that time, comprehend. I knew nothing about the long, painful road the Apaches had traveled to reach Whitetail, nothing about how many of their loved ones had died along the way. When I arrived, everything I knew about the Chiricahuas was based on events depicted in movies, written about in pulp novels, and described in textbooks, all presented from a one-sided and often sensationalized non-Indian perspective. At least I was not alone in my ignorance of the other side. Nothing giving the Chiricahuas' point of view about the battles fought and the awful tragedies that occurred on both sides in the Arizona and New Mexico countryside was in print or on film at the time, or would be published for another twenty to thirty years.

Elbys Hugar recalled those days: "They used to drive us children down from Whitetail and take us to the movies in Ruidoso to see Roy Rogers and Gene Autry fight the Indians. I always wanted to meet those two fellows. Once Gene Autry came to Ruidoso and sang at the library. I saw him. I always wanted to meet John Wayne, too, and that fellow who played Cochise, Jeff Chandler. [That was in *Broken Arrow*, a movie made many years ago.] The movie was made in more of a white way than an Indian way."[2]

American history books written for classroom use told about the Indian wars, of course. A few even described the dramatic decision making in the highest councils of government that led to sending army troops into battle against the "savages." These books, my source of information about Native Americans, complemented the movies of the day by assuming that government policies designed to facilitate the settlement of the West were correct, and that any resistance to them was wrong. So, when I repeated the standard academic material in an attempt to teach the history of our country to the kids, I perpetuated the party line and really did them a disservice.

Undoubtedly my classes would have been much more interesting to my students if I had known more, if I had been able to stand at the blackboard and draw diagrams of the great battles their ancestors had fought and won, or lost, for that matter. At least I would have brought balance to the topic. If impartial educational materials had been available, I could have described the strategic military maneuvers the Apache leaders had utilized to outwit the American troops.

But all of our textbooks were culturally skewed, not just those addressing American history. Texts for teaching the English language pictured neat little New England villages with paved streets and traffic lights controlling busy intersections. Policemen wore blue caps and carried whistles and billy clubs. Milkmen followed their routes, and garbage collectors made their appointed rounds. White-steepled churches competed with shops, factories, and office buildings for space. Blond, blue-eyed fathers in overalls or business suits went off to work with their lunch buckets or briefcases, climbing aboard city buses or hailing cabs. Odd as it seemed to me, I was forced to explain an entire foreign culture to the kids before I could begin teaching the English language.

If I had known even the basics of Chiricahua culture I would have told the kids about the skillful way traditional homes called wickiups were built by Apache women utilizing only branches and boughs, or about the way moccasins were cut and sewn to last almost indefinitely despite punishing wear across harsh desert and mountain terrain. The students would have heard from a white man how their forebears, the Athapascans, later known as Apaches and Navajos, migrated south from the MacKenzie River valley in western Canada and eventually arrived in what would someday become the southwestern United States. They were late arrivals to the area, having been preceded by a group known initially as the Anasazi, later called the Pueblo peoples.

The Athapascans arrived in the Southwest sometime in the early 1500s. It is said that the Zuni Puebloans gave them their name: *apachu* in the Zuni tongue means "enemy." Through a gradual process of separation, many divisions emerged out of the mass of immigrants. One of these smaller units was named Chiricahua, probably by the Opata Indians of Mexico, according to Edwin Sweeney. Further differentiation among the Chiricahuas produced four bands: the Chihenne, Nedni, Chokonen, and Bedonkohe.[3] The Chokonen is the band more familiarly known in popular culture as the Chiricahuas although the Chiricahua children at Whitetail were descended from all four groups.

Anthropologists, researchers, and historians hold varying opinions about the Chiricahuas and their constituent groups. Morris Opler believed they were divided into three bands:

(1) the eastern band, who resided mainly in the territory west of the Rio Grande in New Mexico and were known variously as the Warm Springs, Mimbres, Coppermine, and Mogollon Apaches;
(2) the central band, who resided in the Dos Cabezas, Chiricahua, Dragoon, Mule, and Huachuca Mountains of Arizona and a small territory in northern Mexico, and were called the Cochise Apaches, in honor of one of their most famous leaders; and
(3) the southern band, who lived in a small portion of southwestern New Mexico and northern Mexico and were called the Nedni, Pinery, and Broncho Apaches.[4]

William B. Griffen wrote that in 1800 the Chiricahua Apaches comprised three groups:

(1) the Chokonen, who lived primarily in the Chiricahua Mountains of Arizona;

(2) the Bedonkohe, who lived north and east of the Chokonen; and

(3) the Nednehi (same as Nedni above), who lived in Mexico in the Sierra Madre.[5]

Max Moorhead concluded that at the close of the eighteenth century there were nine distinct Apache groups: the Navajos, Mimbreños, Gileños, Tontos, and Coyoteros, all living west of the Rio Grande, and the Faraones, Mescaleros, Llaneros, and Lipanes east of the river.[6]

All three authors are at least partially correct. The Apache bands underwent constant fission and fusion. People joined and left groups for reasons related to marriage, family matters, social events, food availability, and many other circumstances. Immediate family or extended family units and their various allegiances often determined the size and nature of groups at any given time. This flow was common within the Apache units not only when they initially arrived in the Southwest, but as time went on and the people became more and more involved with other tribes residing in the same region. By September, 1886, the end of liberty, the Chiricahua band led by Naiche and Geronimo included members of other Apache groups who had survived years of warfare with the Mexican and U.S. armies.

The final capitulation of the powerful Apache nation began in April, 1886. Weary of fighting and running, one group of about seventy Chiricahuas surrendered. Led by Chief Chihuahua, the prisoners were placed on a train in Arizona and sent east to St. Augustine, Florida. On April 14, 1886, in St. Augustine, Chihuahua's Apaches were herded like livestock from the train to Fort Marion, a coquina-shell fortress overlooking the North River. Crossing the drawbridge over the dry moat that surrounded the fort must have been a new and terrifying experience for the Apaches, especially for those who looked over their shoulders and saw the wooden drawbridge rise behind them. Confused, frightened, and angry, the Chiricahuas could do nothing but await their fate, now in the hands of their enemy—the United States government.

This first group of Chiricahua Apache prisoners of war included many who had never lifted a weapon against the United States. In fact, some members of Chihuahua's group were scouts who had helped the soldiers fight their relatives and friends. Nevertheless, the scouts were imprisoned beside those they fought against.

The political procedures leading to the incarceration of the next group of Chiricahua Apaches started three months after Chihuahua's band left Arizona and involved nearly four hundred men, women, and children living on an Arizona reservation among the San Carlos Apaches. Circumstances between the two groups were often uneasy. Blaming the Chiricahuas for the problems, the government considered relocating them, despite the fact that they had become industrious farmers. A delegation of thirteen Chiricahuas, men and women, was summoned from San Carlos to Washington, D.C., to meet with Secretary of War William C. Endicott and to hear about the virtues of living in Indian Territory, now part of the state of Oklahoma. Government officials believed that the group's leader, a former warrior and scout named Chatto, would be so impressed with the effusive description that he would agree to be transferred from Arizona to Oklahoma. The plan was to have Chatto convince his associates and followers still living on the Arizona reservation to join him in the new location, and the problems at San Carlos would be solved. But Chatto told another government official, L. Q. C. Lamar, that he didn't want to leave Arizona, where he and his tribe were happy and productive. Disappointed, Lamar then offered to provide the Apache delegation with more farming implements back home. Chatto was pleased, and the Apaches left Washington believing they had made their point.

On the return trip to Arizona, the thirteen Chiricahuas and their military escort traveled by rail to Carlisle Barracks in Pennsylvania and stopped to visit the Chiricahua Apache children in school there. Then they continued their journey to the Southwest. Within two days of reaching Arizona, the train, under orders, turned and headed east again. At Fort Leavenworth, Kansas, the Apaches were detained as prisoners for nearly two months and finally were told they would not be allowed to return to their homes. On September 12, 1886, Chatto and the twelve others left Fort Leavenworth under guard and were taken by train to Fort Marion, where they were imprisoned with the Chiricahua Apaches from Chihuahua's group.

On the third day after that small delegation arrived at Fort Marion, the largest Apache group to be incarcerated as a unit joined them. The 383 Chiricahua and Warm Springs Apaches who had been living and peacefully farming on the San Carlos Reservation had been rounded up and placed on a train under guard on September 7, 1886. Most had never been on a train before and were hesitant to get aboard. They were rudely assisted by the soldiers. This Atchison, Topeka, and Santa Fe special was composed of twelve cars: ten coaches for the Indians (with all the windows nailed shut and no place to lie down and sleep), and two cars for the eighty-four soldiers and nine officers.[7] Off they went, east from Holbrook, Arizona, to join the others at Fort Marion.

Eugene Chihuahua, son of the chief, greeted his relatives and friends when they arrived in Florida almost two weeks later. "They were almost dead," he said. "They were almost naked, they were hungry, and they were pitifully dirty."[8] No wonder. It had always been their practice to leave a campsite before the buildup and disposal of human wastes became a problem. Living as they did in wickiups built of branches and brush, it was a simple matter to move on when sanitary conditions required it. But of course this was impossible to do on a train, regardless of whether or not it was sealed shut.

Compounding the terrible physical conditions was the fact that many of the uprooted Apaches had not had a chance to bathe or change their clothes before leaving the San Carlos Reservation. To make matters worse, these proud people were humiliated time and time again in the near-carnival atmosphere that prevailed among onlookers in depots where the train stopped in its cross-country trip. Little did the prisoners know that strangers gawking at them would become commonplace in the future, when, with the concurrence of the military, they would be exploited as tourist attractions in Florida and Alabama.

The number of prisoners of war at Fort Marion increased again in October, 1886, with the addition of seventeen or eighteen women and children from the Naiche-Geronimo group. Early in the previous month, the surrender of this infamous band had been accomplished without bloodshed in Skeleton Canyon, Arizona. During the conferences that led to the final capitulation, Gen. Nelson A. Miles promised the men that they would be reunited with their loved ones who were already incarcerated in the East. Although the warriors knew nothing about Florida or about what their imprisonment would entail, they realized that if they continued to resist they would be hunted down and exterminated to the last individual, no matter how long it took. Always the pragmatists, Naiche, Geronimo, and their followers laid down their arms for the last time. The group was taken to Fort Bowie, about sixty miles from the surrender site, and very soon afterward they were put on a train waiting for them in the town of Bowie Station, Arizona. "When they put us on the train at Bowie," recalled Jasper Kanseah, Sr., "nobody thought that we'd get far before they'd stop and kill us."[9]

The train halted for the first time two days later in San Antonio, Texas. Brig. Gen. D. S. Stanley, commanding the Department of Texas at San Antonio, had been instructed by his superiors to take charge of the prisoners and hold them until further orders were issued. They remained in San Antonio until October 20 while long discussions took place in Washington concerning the fate of all the prisoners and a suitable place to keep the warriors. Finally, Lt. Gen. Philip H. Sheridan ordered the train to continue eastward.

But contrary to what they had been given to understand by Lt. Charles Gatewood during the negotiations in Skeleton Canyon—"Surrender and you will be sent with your families to Florida"[10]—the men of the Naiche-Geronimo band were not permitted to accompany their families to Fort Marion. Instead, when the train halted at Jacksonville, Florida, the men were removed from the train while the women and children were sent on to St. Augustine. There is no written record of the warriors' response to this broken promise, but it is known that Naiche and Geronimo regarded "the separation of themselves from their families as a violation of the terms of their treaty of surrender."[11]

The men continued traveling, by train and boat, to Fort Pickens, an abandoned structure on Santa Rosa Island off the coast of Pensacola, three hundred miles away. In November of the same year the last holdouts, Mangus's small group of less than a dozen, surrendered. The men were sent to Fort Pickens, and the women and children were confined in Fort Marion. Thus, at the end of 1886 the entire Chiricahua Apache nation was imprisoned in two Florida fortresses.

At Fort Marion more than five hundred men, women, and children were crowded onto less than an acre of land, forced to live in the open atop the fort in tipis crowded together. They cooked their food over small fires. Most of the food was fish and thus inedible to many prisoners because of ancient Chiricahua taboos. Sanitary facilities were nonexistent on the terreplein; to relieve themselves the Apaches had to descend a wide staircase and use a casemate just off the courtyard. Urine and feces seeped through the sand into the water supply, contaminating the only source of drinking water available to them. Contagious diseases broke out among the Chiricahuas immediately, in some cases brought into the compound by the curious tourists who were permitted to gawk and mingle among them. The first to fall ill were those who arrived as part of the largest group on September 20, 1886. Within the first ten days of incarceration, seventy-six prisoners became sick, sixty with the intermittent fevers of malaria; one woman died. Within three months, at least eighteen men, women, and children were terminally ill, including some from Naiche's band, who had arrived on October 25, 1886, and a few who had surrendered with Mangus, warrior son of Mangas Coloradas, in November.[12]

Things were much better for the men at Fort Pickens. As the only prisoner occupants of the fort, the twenty or so men lived in two casemates that had fireplaces, although most of the cooking was done outdoors. Firewood provided by the army was supplemented with driftwood collected along the beach by the prisoners. It is strange to think of the fearsome Geronimo walking barefoot on the hot, white sand with his trouser legs rolled up, carrying driftwood in his arms. But he and the others were immediately put to work. After years of abandonment the fort was rife with varmints and overrun with weeds, and the once mighty Chiricahua Apache warriors were in the right place at the right time to rid the grounds of unwelcome brush, rats, and snakes. During the first months of their confinement, they also removed a large amount of debris—broken bricks, rotten planks, and stones—that had accumulated in the ditches and on the grounds around the fort. A prolonged drought had lowered the water in the cisterns to a critical point, so when time permitted, the Apache men dug wells among the dunes to get water for cooking and washing.

In early February, 1887, after the hardest cleanup work had been done, tourists were allowed to visit and mingle with the prisoners. Geronimo became a star attraction. Forever crafty, he realized his own popularity and devoted his considerable natural talents to promoting himself. He sold souvenirs to the tourists: trinkets he had carved from driftwood, buttons from his clothing, even his mark on a piece of paper. The warriors quickly adjusted to their new roles of quasi celebrities and gracious hosts to large parties of curious sightseers. Yet, despite their exposure to thousands of excursionists and the damp and humid climate, and despite the severe disruption in their natural lifestyle, none of the Apache men at Fort Pickens became seriously ill.

At Fort Marion, meanwhile, the death toll kept rising and the news media began to take notice. After the deaths received nationwide publicity, the country began to demand relief for the prisoners. In the spring of 1887, to quiet the public clamor, the surviving prisoners were moved from St. Augustine to Mount Vernon, Alabama, thirty miles north of Mobile.

Geronimo and the other men joined them from Fort Pickens shortly thereafter.

The new prison camp in Alabama, where the Chiricahuas spent the next eight years, was no better than Fort Marion. Many more prisoners fell ill. There was very little circulation of air in the hollow where they lived, and insufficient rations were a problem. To add to their meager diet, the men were permitted to walk under guard along the railroad tracks and look for cows that had been hit by the trains. If they could drag the carcasses back to the prison camp, they had meat. Contagious diseases were still rampant, complicated by ailments and deaths caused by self-medication with unfamiliar plant medicines. In 1894, when public outrage over the medical catastrophes brought about the end of the Alabama stay, approximately three hundred Chiricahuas lay in unmarked graves in the woods surrounding the prison camp. The surviving prisoners, numbering a little more than two hundred, were transferred once again, this time to Fort Sill, Oklahoma. After several more years of continued illnesses, a plateau of sorts was reached, and the number of dying Apaches decreased. Recovery was slow, but the resilient men, women, and children made a comeback over the next twenty years.

In 1913 and 1914, after many years of debate within the government, the incarceration finally came to an end. Congress ordered the prisoners to be released, although they were given a choice between only two places to settle: they must either remain in the area around Fort Sill or go to the Mescalero Apache Reservation in New Mexico. Eighty-nine Chiricahuas chose to remain in Oklahoma, and 187 elected to go west. Whitetail, a remote area of the reservation, was chosen as the location for the freed Chiricahuas. In April, 1913, they arrived, thirty-five years before I did.

Totally ignorant of what the Chiricahuas had endured and survived, in my one-room classroom at Whitetail I taught Geronimo's kids American history, including the "fact" that the Indians of the Southwest had to be subdued by every means possible so that the settlers, the miners, the ranchers, the sheep farmers, the adventurers, the missionaries, and everyone else who wanted the Apache homelands could live peacefully on the land.

If only I had known . . .

Chapter 4
The Old Timers at Whitetail

As I look back at a time nearly fifty years past, I realize how fortunate I was to associate with the Chiricahuas on their own turf. Not many white people had that opportunity—only several teachers, a handful of missionaries, and some Bureau of Indian Affairs personnel. We were the chosen few, in my opinion, privileged to share a unique experience: living and working amid the sons and daughters of the Chiricahua Apache nation. My only regret is that I was so young then and still untutored in the true history of the people around me, and I never fully understood or appreciated each day's happenings. But I have fond memories, some still quite vivid, and I have numerous recollections of individual Apaches, all of whom apparently were related in one way or another.

The Chiricahua Apache kinship system, including the terminology that reflects connections, is so extensive that it is beyond the scope of this book. Briefly, however, there are seven principal features illuminated by nomenclature:

(1) All terms except parent-child relationships are reciprocal, and a Chiricahua addresses his relatives as they address him;
(2) Four separate terms are used for each grandparent, and a grandparent's siblings are classified with the grandparent;
(3) There is a separate term for mother, but her siblings are classified under one term;
(4) A father is addressed by a separate terms, but his siblings are classified under one term;
(5) There are separate terms for stepfather and stepmother;

(6) No distinction is made between siblings, parallel cousins, or cross-cousins;

(7) Only true children are called son and daughter.

Despite the use of kinship terminology, most Chiricahuas are well aware of blood connections and more remote affiliations. The term "cousin" is today very popular and serves as an umbrella under which many people stand. For example, Mildred Cleghorn, the former chairperson of the Fort Sill Chiricahua/Warm Springs Apache Tribe in Apache, Oklahoma, calls Kathleen Kanseah of the Mescalero Apache Reservation her "cousin." Mrs. Cleghorn's paternal grandparents, Go-la-ah-tsa and her husband Clee-neh, are Mrs. Kanseah's paternal great-grandparents (that is, Cleghorn's father and Kanseah's paternal grandmother were brother and sister).

As another example, Geronimo thought of Ishton as his "sister," but it is probable that she was his cousin. The distinction did not matter. Her son was Asa Daklugie, later one of the Chiricahua leaders at Whitetail, who has always been thought of as Geronimo's nephew.

One of my friends at Whitetail was Robert Geronimo, the only surviving true son of the famous shaman and warrior. There can be no doubt about Robert's ancestry; he looked just like his father.

Robert Geronimo

In 1909, four years before the Chiricahuas first set foot in Whitetail, eighty-year-old Geronimo died in Oklahoma, still a prisoner of war. His death was unexpected, for despite his advanced age, the infamous old Apache was in reasonably good health. On a cold, rainy February day, with the army's permission, Geronimo rode his pony off the Fort Sill military reserve into the nearby town of Lawton. Enjoying his excursion, the old warrior drank too much, and on the way back he toppled off his horse. Geronimo lay out in the open all that night as the rain fell in sheets. When a search party found him the next morning, they rushed him immediately to the Apache hospital on the grounds of Fort Sill. But pneumonia set in quickly, and the legendary warrior died several days later.

Geronimo's demise from "natural causes" was not a very exciting ending to a life so full of high drama. It is possible, however, that the old warrior had had some idea of how he would die. Geronimo had always been aware of his destiny, the result of an event that happened in his younger days. In the winter of 1869–70 he traveled a great distance and risked his life to be with Ishton, whose pregnancy was near term. During her difficult childbirth, Geronimo became fearful that she would die. Deeply concerned, he left her side to pray alone for her life atop a nearby peak. "As he lifted his hands and eyes toward the east," wrote author Angie Debo, "his Power spoke: 'The child will be born and your sister will live; and you will never be killed with weapons, but live to an old age.'"[1] For the rest of his life Geronimo trusted his Power's words, and he was never betrayed. Hundreds of bullets whizzed by him, but most missed their mark. He coordinated and participated in daring escapes and was chased by armies; he endured nearly thirty years of incarceration under physical conditions that took the lives of nearly half of all the Chiricahua Apaches imprisoned with him. Still he lived, believing in his Power's promise.

Until the latter years of Geronimo's life he did not know his son Robert very well. The boy was reared by his mother, a Mescalero Apache woman named Ih-tedda, who is said to have been about fourteen years old when she became Geronimo's seventh wife in late 1885. According to Gillett Griswold,[2] Ih-tedda was visiting the White Mountain/San Carlos Apache reservation in Arizona when Geronimo spirited her away in late 1885 during one of his numerous escapes. She traveled with him and the others in the Naiche-Geronimo band until the group surrendered nearly one year later. Ih-tedda was confined with the Chiricahuas at Fort Marion, Florida, and Mount Vernon, Alabama, where the couple lived together until 1889, when the authorities permitted Ih-tedda (who was not a Chiricahua by birth) and her two small children, daughter Lenna and newborn son Robert, to return to her home, the Mescalero Apache Reservation in New Mexico. In the Apache way, this separation was equivalent to divorce, and, as was customary, Ih-tedda remarried soon afterward.

Eve Ball offered another version of Ih-tedda's departure from Mount Vernon. According to Ball, Ih-tedda begged to remain with her husband in the Alabama prison camp, but Geronimo said, "Any minute we may all be shot. There is no reason why you and our daughter should lose your lives. You must return to Mescalero."[3] Ih-tedda and a few others freed along with her then went by train to New Mexico, accompanied by a soldier and his wife. In Ball's account, Ih-tedda was not visibly pregnant when she left the prison camp to join her family at Mescalero. According to tradition, the family quickly married her, against her wishes, to Old Cross Eyes, a retired scout. From then on she was called Katie Cross Eyes. When her son was born, she registered him at the Mescalero agency as Robert Cross Eyes, and fifteen years later, when Robert entered the Indian school at Chilocco, Oklahoma Territory, he still carried that name. Later, however, Ih-tedda requested that his name be officially changed to Robert Geronimo.

Other interpretations of Robert's personal history exist, including one that says he was born on the train en route from Alabama to New Mexico. Another places Robert's birth sometime after his mother and older sister arrived in New Mexico. Robert himself told me that he was born on August 2, 1889, in Alabama, and that the record of his birth was kept in the Indian agency office at Mescalero, which burned in 1902 and again in 1908. He also said that, in addition to Lenna and himself, Ih-tedda had two other children by Geronimo, a boy and a girl, but they died in infancy before Robert was born.

Robert was sent from Mescalero to Chilocco in about 1905, and his father visited him there that year. It was their first acquaintance with each other, and it came just four years before the old man died. Robert remained at Chilocco a little more than two years and spent his summers at Fort Sill with Geronimo. They developed a close relationship, and Geronimo accepted Robert without question as his son; the facial resemblance between the two is striking. Robert told me that he learned much from his father, but he never said exactly what it was that he learned, and by the time he felt free enough to talk with me at all, I knew enough not to probe. The Chiricahuas grow uncomfortable under direct questioning, and I always let them talk at their own pace. To do otherwise would have been self-defeating; they never would have told me another thing.

At the end of the 1907 school year Robert joined Geronimo in Oklahoma. Although he lived among the Apache prisoners of war, he was never considered to be a captive himself, and the government never restricted his activities.

Robert stayed at Fort Sill until 1910, when, at his own request, he was sent to Carlisle School for more education. He lived in Pennsylvania for about four years, working on local farms during the summers. He visited Fort Sill again in 1912. I recall him talking about his years at Carlisle, and he seemed proud to be a graduate but not completely happy about what happened there. I could only imagine what he meant. Later, much later, I learned about the tuberculosis that was rampant at Carlisle, and I assume Robert's references and unhappiness reflected that.

In 1913, when the Chiricahua prisoners of war who opted to live on the Mescalero Apache Reservation were freed, Robert was listed in absentia on the census form. One year later, on the release of the remaining Chiricahuas from incarceration, he was counted among those who chose to remain in Oklahoma. Robert received an allotment of almost 158 acres of farmland in Oklahoma, but in 1914 he made Whitetail his permanent home. Always vague about what hurt him the most, Robert spoke little to me about his land in Oklahoma, saying only that it was "in question." He said he planned to talk with one of the U.S. senators from New Mexico to have the matter straightened out, but he did not keep me informed.

Robert's first wife was Ester Rodriguez, a sixteen-year-old Lipan Apache woman who had been brought from Mexico to Mescalero when she was a small child. Ester had a past history of tuberculosis and had been warned by doctors not to have children. Nonetheless, Robert fell in love with her and wanted to marry her and start a family. In January, 1917, Father Albert Braun, O.F.M., performed the wedding ceremony in the Saint Joseph's Catholic mission at Mescalero. Robert paid for Ester's wedding dress and bought a new suit for the occasion with his savings. At the church, he realized that he had left his fancy new shoes at home in Whitetail, and complained to the priest that it was too far to go to claim them. The priest consoled Robert by saying, "That's all right . . . Ester is not marrying your shoes."[4] He was married in the shoes he was wearing—cowboy boots.

Ester and Robert Geronimo eventually became the parents of three girls, none of whom caused their mother's death in childbirth, as had been predicted. Sadly, however, Ester did die young. According to Chiricahua kinship tradition, Robert then married her sister, Juanita Rodriguez, and that union produced three more children.[5]

Robert's third wife was Maude Daklugie, daughter of Asa Daklugie and granddaughter of Chief Juh, of the Nedni Apaches, and of Chief Chihuahua, of the Chiricahuas. Robert and Maude had no children, and the marriage was eventually dissolved. "We were both past fifty when we were married," Maude Geronimo told Eve Ball. "My father liked Robert but he made us get a divorce. He did it because he believed Robert to be Geronimo's son, not Cross Eyes'. And the marriage of close relatives is forbidden. His mother [Maude's grandmother] was a sister [first cousin] of Geronimo. That made Robert and me cousins. We had to obey him. He was more than my father; he was my chief. I have been very lonely and unhappy. Now my father is gone, but Robert and I can never remarry."[6]

Robert's mother, Ih-tedda, was cared for in the Public Health Service hospital at Mescalero after Cross Eyes died. At that time there were no homes for the elderly on the reservation. Before she died in 1952, Ih-tedda spoke with Eve Ball through an Apache interpreter and gave a brief but concise account of her abduction from the Arizona reservation by Geronimo, of her marriages to him and to Cross Eyes, and of Robert.[7] Although I never met Ih-tedda, "Katie Cross Eyes," I feel that I became acquainted with her through Robert's descriptions.

Robert and I became pals rather quickly, which was unusual, and not long after I met him he began to air his opinions and speak more or less freely with me. For example, during one particular jocular moment Robert confided that the only reason Apaches wore feathers was because the "white eyes" thought that all Indians wore them. He said his father sometimes wore feathers in public to please the tourists, and that the old man often did crazy things to take a few dollars away from any white visitors. He also said that Geronimo traveled a lot at government expense and allowed the United States to use him to "advertise" its victory over the Chiricahua Apaches. According to Robert, though, Geronimo played it for all he could, believing that his public appearances worked for the good of the tribe. How? Robert said Geronimo thought that after seeing him, people would know how harmless (!) he was and would hear of the suffering the Apaches had endured.

Robert also said that Geronimo laughed quite a lot and was mean only after he had had a few drinks. Still, who can forget the familiar photos of Geronimo, his mouth a slash across his face, his eyes glaring into the camera? I have never seen a photo of Geronimo smiling. I wonder if one exists. During that same conversation, Robert admitted that the "scalps" on a belt Geronimo wore in one photo were really animal pelts, adding that the Apaches were repulsed by the idea of taking scalps. Although I believed him without question at the time, through the years I have heard or read mixed comments about scalping by the Chiricahuas. In an interview with author Angie Debo on January 26, 1955, Jason Betzinez (one of Geronimo's relatives) said he had heard of an incident where an Apache woman took revenge on a Mexican who had scalped her son, killing him. And Asa Daklugie, son of Nedni chief Juh told Eve Ball that occasionally an Apache took a scalp but thereafter had to undergo a purification ceremony. Judging from these reports, I concluded that scalpings by the Chiricahuas were isolated incidents and that the myth of Geronimo wearing a blanket of nearly one hundred scalps was just that—a myth.

Old Timers ✦ 51

Robert's physical likeness to his father was a trait I noticed immediately when I first saw him, a week or two after I arrived at Whitetail. I'll never forget that day. I was at the tribal store and had just loaded groceries and a few other supplies into the school bus. I was just about ready to leave for Whitetail when one of the men lounging in front of the place called, "Wait a minute!" A heavyset Apache with his belt at low tide waddled toward me, huffing and wheezing and aiming a finger down the gravel road that led to the highway. "Maude and Robert want a ride out to Whitetail," he said when he caught his breath. "How will I know them?" I asked. "The only ones there," he replied. "He's the son of the big chief Geronimo. You better watch out!" He really played the role for the new white teacher.

One of the characteristics of the Chiricahuas that I had noticed immediately was their love of the outdoors and of walking. It was normal for Whitetail residents to walk down the mountain to the center of Mescalero and back, a twenty-seven mile jaunt each way. When I saw couples walking, often the man, empty-handed, proceeded about ten paces ahead of his wife. His wife walked dutifully behind, lugging whatever needed to be carried. I thought this was terrible, but I learned much later that it was customary behavior based on years of tradition. In the old days when the Chiricahuas were free, men were expected to be out in front of the women and children, carrying weapons at the ready to protect them. A man's job was to literally risk his life for his family. If any danger appeared, the wife would be warned by her husband's actions well enough in advance to run and hide. He parried and diverted the attack or paid the ultimate price for his bravery. Not too long ago when Henrietta Stockel and a Chiricahua family were hiking along the path to Arizona's Fort Bowie, she noticed that the eldest son was in the lead, followed by the women, and the father brought up the rear. The family had slipped into their traditional ways without saying a word about it.

I saw another example of women's roles later, when my parents were visiting us at Whitetail. A sloppy wet day with melting snow had turned the teacherage driveway into a rutty, slippery mess. A freeze a few days earlier had caused pipes to burst, and families left without water had to come to the school to get it. Our pipes were buried and otherwise protected from temperature fluctuations, and there was a public tap for just such occasions.

On this particular winter day, a vintage Nash full of Apache men and one Apache woman, the driver, slithered down our drive and sank in the mud right near an outside faucet. The woman got out and, unassisted, filled the water jugs they had brought. After loading them back in the trunk, she tried to drive away. No luck. Her spinning rear wheels threw mud about fifteen feet back up the drive, almost splattering the teacherage, as they tried to bite into drier earth. The car only sank deeper into the mire. The men reluctantly got out and slogged around the car, discussing strategy. Unable to reach a conclusion, they reentered the car and assumed their former seats beside and in back of the woman driver. Then everyone got out again. And then, to my father's astonishment, all the men got back into the car, one of them behind the wheel. The woman quietly walked to the back of the car and began trying to push the fully loaded vehicle out of the mud. Eventually she moved it. Covered with mud, she got back behind the wheel after the male driver moved over. Then they drove away. "Wow!" shouted my father. "Wait until I tell the fellows about that!" I quickly pushed him inside the house and gave him his first lesson in how to respond to differences in local customs, if you want to survive among the Apaches without being embarrassed by your outburst, that is. (Interestingly, I visited Whitetail in August, 1993, with Berle Kanseah, son of Jasper Kanseah, Jr., shortly after a drenching mountain rain. Our car, believe it or not, got stuck in the exact same place. After we had a good laugh, he pushed me out.)

Not very many non-Apaches are familiar with traditional women's roles within the Chiricahua culture, including the fact that they were expected to be subordinate to their husbands. In the time before incarceration women were also expected to gather food, plant and irrigate and harvest the crops, provide and prepare large amounts of food for extended family members, build protective shelters, and give birth to healthy babies.

One important job of a Chiricahua woman was to pray every morning for four days after the men left on a hunt. She was also expected to teach her children how to pray, not only for their father's success in bringing back a generous supply of food, but for the health and well being of everyone in the tribe. Children who remained around their mothers learned quickly about the connections between prayer and Apache spirituality and also learned about the taboos. For example, when the men returned from a hunt, a pregnant wife would not eat the intestines or calves of a deer's leg, for if she did, it was believed that her husband's arrows would not follow a straight path the next time he went hunting.

In most of a husband and wife's actions together, the husband and his wishes and needs dominated. As an example, after the wife prepared a meal, her husband ate first; her meal consisted of whatever he left. She was expected to bring him his horse and saddle and carry water for the family in a large bottle she wove of grasses and reeds. The vessel was smeared with pine pitch, inside and out, to make it watertight. She carried the bottle on her back and supported it by a strap across her forehead.

If a wife offended her husband in any way, she could expect to be beaten by him, but her family had a right to intervene and protect her. A woman who committed adultery ran the risk of having her nose cut off at its tip by an enraged husband, if she were caught. If he failed to punish her in this way, he lost face among members of his band, and if an Apache man lost face for any reason, his shame and humiliation were great.

By 1948 a good many of these customs were no longer in existence. However, women still frequently deferred to their husbands, but individual family variations were appearing. A number of the women at Whitetail had been educated at Carlisle School and participated in the "outing system," an integral part of that learning experience. Conceived by Superintendent Richard Henry Pratt, the outing system placed girls (and boys) in private white homes where the students were expected to become more fluent in the English language, acquire domestic skills, and generally be exposed to another culture. Sadly, the program was abused at many locations and became a means of providing servants to households before it was discontinued. Importantly, though, the education Apache girls received at Carlisle, along with experiences in the outing program, caused many of them to reject traditional Chiricahua women's roles in favor of more equitable and modern behavior.

Still today, however, pockets of the old ways remain. When Henrietta Stockel attended a Chiricahua celebration in Apache, Oklahoma, a few years ago, she ate dinner with a medicine man and half a dozen male members of his entourage. Noticing that the medicine man's coffee cup was empty, one of the men turned to her and instructed, "Get him another cup of coffee." Stockel, a very modern and independent woman, got the message: the traditional Apache men expected her to wait on them because she was the only woman present. Waiting only a few seconds to compose herself, she rose from the table and did as directed, muttering to herself all the way to the coffee urn and back to the table.

But, back to my first meeting with Robert Geronimo. He and his wife were sitting beside the main reservation road, content to stay there for as long as it took to catch a ride home. Admittedly, I was a little uneasy when I spotted them. They looked younger than they actually were. The man was stocky, and his wife looked as if she were round. A bandanna covered her head. Both looked very dignified. I pulled over and was about to get out and help them get in, but they had already opened the door on the passenger side and were climbing into the bus as though they had been expecting me. I turned, introduced myself as the new teacher at Whitetail, and got nods and silence in return. We drove a while before Robert suddenly said, "I'm Robert. This is my wife, Maude." He gave no last name. "Good to know you," I said, and we drove on.

No one talked. When we reached the unmarked turn to Whitetail, I asked if it was the right road. Robert nodded his head and pointed. Still we made no conversation. The main highway was soon lost in the background beyond the trees as the bus pushed along the road, huge plumes of gravel dust billowing behind. Occasionally I slowed down to squeeze through tight spaces where a few tall pines guarded the way, their branches forming giant arches overhead. We forged on, going no more than ten miles per hour, hugging the hillsides and straddling the ruts.

In the rearview mirror I could see my passengers' solemn, placid faces staring straight ahead. To be honest, I was uncertain of my safety with them, and just as I was starting to worry seriously about that, Robert came suddenly alive, his eyes ablaze. "Stop the bus!" he shouted. I slammed on the brakes, and almost before we could squeak and grind to a halt, Robert was out the door. He ran back down the road and retrieved something from a ditch, then hurried to the bus, clutching an object to his breast. As he jumped aboard, a smile broke over his face. He turned to Maude and then to me, cramming an old hat on his head. Only his ears kept it above his eyes. The smile vanished as he lifted it off his head, turning it over in his hands and sadly examining it. Then he shrugged. "Oh, well. It'll be good for my horse," he said as he began to poke two holes in the brim for horse ears. "This is a good hat," he declared. "It's a Stetson." After that icebreaker our conversation flowed.

After we were better acquainted, Robert would drop over often and sit on the teacherage porch telling tales of his childhood. As a youth growing up on the Mescalero Apache Reservation, Robert would rise on cold winter mornings, dress in little more than a loincloth, grab a bucket, and run through the snow to the creek. He would break the thin ice with his bare feet by jumping right into it, fill the bucket, and run back to the family's wickiup. He said that he never got sick until he started to wear heavy sheepskin winter coats like the white men wear.

Robert and Maude lived within view of the teacherage, about half a mile away over open fields. To visit them I would drive along the dirt road and negotiate a sharp right-hand bend. They lived in the first house on the right after that. It was set back a bit from the road and was usually festooned with fragrant strips of beef jerky and red chile peppers (*ristras* in Spanish) hanging from strings. The colorful display always reminded me of Christmas decorations.

Inside the house, a huge sepia-toned photograph dominated the back wall of the living room. It was an enlargement of the familiar picture of Geronimo crouching, wearing his scalp belt, and with his rifle leaning on his shoulder. I thought he had a stern, bloodthirsty look in his eyes. "That's my daddy," Robert said proudly, the first time I stared in awe at the face of the infamous Apache. "I remember when that picture was taken," Robert added. "A photographer came to the stockade one day and paid the soldiers some money. Then he paid my father to pose for him. Daddy was laughing because the scalp locks were 'coons' tails, but the photographer told him to look serious. So he scowled just as the flash powder went off. Then he started to laugh again."

Robert's father-in-law and mother-in-law, Asa and Ramona Daklugie, lived in the next house down the road beyond Robert's. On one visit to Robert and Maude, I asked if I could go next door to visit Asa. Maude cautioned me that her father wanted nothing to do with white people, but I didn't understand it at the time. It was only later, after I had learned more about the circumstances behind the U.S. government's imprisonment of the Chiricahua Apaches, that I understood Asa's hatred. Still, Asa's wife, Ramona, had been through the same agony and was a warm and friendly woman. It was a puzzle. The longer I thought about it, the more I realized that forgiveness was a trait most of the Chiricahuas shared. They taught me much of what I know about understanding, excusing, and pardoning. In my personal life, whenever the occasion warrants, I still try to call forth the remarkable charity and grace I saw in the hearts of most Chiricahuas in the years that I knew them.

When not working in the fields around his house at Whitetail, Robert would sit and whittle bows and arrows to be sold to tourists at the tribal store. His work was fine craftsmanship. He began by carefully selecting a young sapling for the bow and tying it down so that it formed just the right arch. Once shaped, it would grow in that position until it was ready to be harvested, after which it was dried and aged. When the time was right, Robert used an old piece of tin can as a rasp or rough file to sculpt the bow. Beef or deer tendon was the string. Each step was an art and took an amazingly long time. I often wondered if the tourists who bought these artifacts for a pittance ever appreciated the effort and skill that went into making them. Oddly, when he hunted wild game at Whitetail, Robert never used a bow and arrows. He carried an old .30-.30 held together with bailing wire. The stock had broken one day during a hunting trip, and he had no equipment to fix it. Considering how particular he was about his bows and arrows, I thought the way he treated his rifle was rather strange. This seemingly contradictory trait of his pops into my memory off and on, usually when I pass a gun store or sporting goods shop.

At those times and many others, and especially right now, I miss Robert Geronimo. Whenever I do, I go and look at his picture, the one I took of him sitting on the stoop of the teacherage. For the last forty years or so it has hung on the wall in my study. You see, Robert Geronimo has traveled with me literally and figuratively throughout my life.

In the summer of 1993 I visited the Mescalero Apache Reservation several times to look up old friends and reacquaint myself with Whitetail. In July, while I was watching a dance put on by Indians from Oklahoma, a dignified, rather slender woman with her hair in a bandanna approached me and crowded in beside me. Since there was very little standing room around the large drum, I stepped aside just slightly to make room for her. When I looked at her, I said, "You look familiar. Are you from Whitetail?" Clearly surprised, she answered, "I'm Robert Geronimo's daughter. He was the son of Geronimo." Her name is Ouida.

I stopped staring at her after a few long seconds and asked her to stay where she was for a just a moment. Then I went to my car to get a publication that had been printed nearly forty years ago before the 1950 puberty ceremony. Ouida Geronimo's photo is on the cover of that book, published by the tribe and called *The Mescalero Apache Tribes Presents The Debut of Its Most Honored Maidens*. As the photo demonstrates, she was a lovely teenager in her ceremonial buckskins.

When I showed her the book, she was amazed. "Where did you get this?" she asked. I admitted that I had been the teacher at Whitetail, and Ouida's smile filled her face. She asked for a copy, explaining that hers had been lost in a move to a new home. I made her a copy later, but first I went back to my car and found an eight-by-ten photo of Robert Geronimo that I had made years ago and just happened to have with me. I gave it to her, and she spontaneously hugged me in thanks.

The Chiricahua Apaches have opened so many doors to me after they learned who I am and realized that I share a part of their past. It has been a humbling experience.

Eugene Chihuahua

Eugene Chihuahua was a lad of about ten when his father, one of the Chiricahua Apaches' leaders, surrendered in March, 1885, six months before the Naiche-Geronimo band did. During the last twenty years of the Apaches' imprisonment, Eugene saw most of his family, including his father, two brothers, two sisters, six children, his mother-in-law, and several other close relatives, die at Fort Sill. Two half sisters had died before then, in Alabama.

Young Eugene was not forced to attend Carlisle School with most of the other Apache children. As a courtesy, the U.S. government gave Eugene's father, Chief Chihuahua, a choice: he could keep one of his children with him in captivity, but the rest had to be sent away to school. The chief chose Eugene, and so the boy remained behind, growing up in confinement in circumstances totally different from his peers. Perhaps it was his very different experiences, along with his heritage, that led Eugene Chihuahua to become a respected leader at Whitetail.

Eugene's first wife was Viola Ziah. Their eight children were all born into captivity; only two lived to accompany them to Mescalero, where Viola died. Eugene remarried twice, once to a Comanche and once to Jennie, a Mescalero Apache. His sister Ramona was Asa Daklugie's wife.

I remember Eugene as a dignified, friendly man who spoke slowly and weighed his words well. He was a renowned medicine man whose healing abilities and knowledge helped many Chiricahuas recover from mild to serious ailments. In our conversations Eugene never hesitated to recall the old days. He loved to tell me about the huge area the Apaches had wandered and claimed as their own. During one discussion he mentioned that Chihuahua, Mexico, had been named for his father, the chief.

Along with his brother-in-law Asa Daklugie, Eugene provided author Eve Ball with invaluable information about the Chiricahua way of life and about himself. For example, he did not hesitate to say that he regretted being one of those responsible for leading his people from Fort Sill to the Mescalero Apache Reservation. His second thoughts were based on his belief that few of the Apaches cared about their farms at Whitetail. I noticed that as well. The community tractor driver did all the plowing and planting, and many of the Apaches let their plots become overgrown with weeds until harvest time.

The older folks, many of whom had been prisoners of war, did most of the hard farm work because the younger ones, those who had been born at Whitetail, refused. Farming just was not in their genes, I guess. Many were good cowboys, and a few became loggers, but they clearly were never interested in tilling the soil. Eugene Chihuahua recognized that and told me he thought the reason might be that his people lacked discipline. The young people were not trained for any work off the reservation and had very little opportunity to use their own initiative. In my opinion, their dependency was fostered on purpose so they would never leave the reservation. Oddly, the few who did manage to leave and make their way in the outside world seemed to feel some shame attached to their success.

But life certainly was not all bleak for the younger generation. Two occupations seemed to generate particular pride: fighting forest fires and serving in the U.S. military. I was fortunate enough to train with the Apache fire fighters for a couple of days. (The crews were just being organized as I was leaving Whitetail.) My assignment was with the shovel crew. Ahead of us were a pick-ax team and a group chopping out shrubs and small trees. My group came along next, throwing loose dirt around to make a firebreak. The whole team had a nice picnic in the woods between rounds, and I remember smelling like a smoked herring. I also remember being all done in by the end of the day. I was not in shape at all! Fortunately for everyone, I did not stay on with them. Maybe that is one reason why today the Mescalero Hot Shots are today among the finest forest-fire fighters in the nation.

Insofar as the military was concerned, serving in the armed forces symbolically continued the warrior tradition. Through the years many Chiricahua Apache men and women have distinguished themselves in all branches of the service.

I remember Eugene telling me that the Chiricahua Apaches liked their western-style homes at Whitetail. They had grown accustomed to the amenities introduced from the outside world and consequently were growing soft. At the same time, though, he seemed to scoff at the Mescalero Apaches who lived down the mountain in tipis or other shelters while their livestock wandered in and out of the government-supplied houses. In truth, there was no real alternative to adopting the white man's ways. No one could turn back the hands of time to the days when the Apaches roamed the Southwest, even though Eugene and others often spoke longingly of the old days of freedom.

No one I knew ever talked about the Chiricahuas' twenty-seven years as prisoners of war, although Eugene talked vaguely about traveling to Mexico to see a few Apaches who had avoided incarceration. It is said that six men, women, and children from Geronimo's band escaped from the caravan of prisoners that left Skeleton Canyon for Fort Bowie under armed military guard after the last surrender. The full story of these "lost" Apaches has never been published, but it has been passed on in oral tradition. I have been told by several Apaches that from time to time, members of this group came back from Mexico to see their relatives. Rumor has it that they camped out in the brush and that some Chiricahuas went back and forth to the Sierra Madre with them. Some researchers, including Eve Ball and her colleagues, looked into the story, but too much time had passed and it was no longer possible to positively identify any descendants of the original Sierra Madre Apaches.

Levi Hosetosewit

Levi Hosetosewit was one of Eugene Chihuahua's stepsons, the son of Eugene's second wife, a Comanche. She later divorced Eugene and moved back to Oklahoma, but Levi and his brothers remained at Whitetail and lived among the Apaches. Levi was the school's bus driver and jack-of-all-trades. Unlike the saying, though, he was the master of many, particularly the care and maintenance of the two official school vehicles at Whitetail. Every week or so I drove down the mountain to Mescalero in either the school's venerable green pickup truck or the old school bus. Levi accompanied me in the truck on my very first trip. The pickup was used to haul supplies and to carry kids when the bus failed to start in the mornings, a frequent occurrence, but this time it was strictly for transportation. Levi and I planned to bring back the old orange Chevy Carryall school bus with black fenders, perhaps of 1936 or 1937 vintage, which had been laid up in the agency garage while extra seats were shoehorned in. These had to be installed in such a way that they could be removed (courtesy of Levi's hard work) to increase the bus's capacity even more. Double the number of children could be crammed in if they all sat on the floor, or in each other's laps, or hung out the windows and doors. If there were any safety regulations governing the use or abuse of school buses in those days, they surely were not in effect on the reservation.

Before we started out, the garage had phoned to let us know that the bus was ready, or at least able to be driven. It had also needed major reconstruction because a former driver had mistaken a can of clear varnish for oil and had dumped it in. Each part of the engine had been removed and washed in a solvent by hand, but the bus still seized up from time to time as the varnish migrated up from deep, unreachable recesses.

Prior to this excursion, Levi and I had not had much of a chance to talk, and I really looked forward to getting to know him and hearing about his wife and young children, who were not yet old enough for school. Levi proved to be a loquacious and funny fellow. About thirty years old, he had a pock-marked face and tousled black hair. His major asset was his willingness to please, which made his shortcomings much more bearable.

Levi needed no encouragement to talk, and he had no problem keeping up his end of the conversation as the pickup twisted and turned down the narrow gravel road. I learned later that Levi had also wanted to impress me with his driving abilities. He did.

The twenty-seven mile trip to the garage seemed shorter with Levi's friendly company. We picked up the old bus after the usual warnings from the mechanic, who sounded like a country doctor giving advice about an ailing patient. On the way back I traveled alone because I had to complete some business and pick up a few groceries before leaving. I missed the pleasure of Levi's company, but I thought it out of character for me to become dependent on someone else's chatter so soon. Little did I know how much all the Chiricahua Apache people would come to mean to me.

Levi was also the custodian of the school and its grounds. He kept the premises clean and repaired broken windows, chairs, and desks. I soon discovered, however, that he was fairly undependable. Worse, I never knew when he would skip work until he failed to show up. In time I learned that Levi often had a run-in with a bottle or two of booze and sometimes did not recover sufficiently by morning to come to work. Levi drove the bus only for a couple of months, and then, out of necessity, I had to find another driver. It was my first difficult personnel decision, because by then I was quite fond of him. While Levi was still employed, an incident occurred that showed me what he could do when he was sober. About two weeks after my wife and I moved in, the wall in the kitchen of the teacherage felt very hot. The bathroom wall on the opposite side was also warm, yet there was no chimney running between them. Pretending to know what I was doing, I skipped down the stairs to the basement. I smelled wood burning, went outside for a look from another angle, and noticed the electric meter spinning wildly. After telling Levi, I jumped in the pickup and flew down to the agency, not bothering to try the telephone; everyone knew it was out of order. I tore into the office and shouted excitedly that the teacherage at Whitetail was on fire. A Mr. Thompkins was in charge at the time, and he calmly showed me the plans for the teacherage. He seemed quite puzzled by my anxiety. When I pointed to the affected area, he called in another worker and they started arguing over whether or not it could be the wiring. I interrupted their discussion to ask how to get in touch with the fire department. There was no fire department.

I ran out the door, jumped into the old bus, and lurched back up to Whitetail. When I arrived, I found a huge hole burned in the roof, and the kitchen wall had been hacked out, revealing charred timbers. I learned that in my absence Levi had gone to a local gravel pit and drafted a few volunteers, who rushed to the scene. The first thing they discovered was that the fire hose, which lay neatly coiled in a wood box in the front yard, was rotted through and through. It exploded when the water was turned on. Levi turned off the power, which had been feeding the fires, and then organized the group into an old-fashioned bucket brigade: passing buckets of water hand to hand. They succeeded in putting out the blaze.

For the longest time a tarp covered the hole in the roof. Then one day an Apache man (I have forgotten his name) appeared to fix the hole in the roof and repaint the teacherage. As this fellow worked, he unselfconciously sang traditional Apache songs. One was delivered with a flourish of sorts, and I was impressed with his voice and the song. In answer to my question, he said it was a love song. Paying me no mind whatsoever, he launched into another melody on the spot, singing as if he were on the Broadway stage. This one was an old war chant, he explained, and then laughed at me when I said I thought there was no difference.

One evening after a long day's work the painter rushed back to the teacherage, clearly in a panic and looking terrified. He said one of the women in his family had gone crazy and tried to attack him with a knife. Believing he needed protection, I offered to let him spend the night in the teacherage, but he only wanted to sit and talk awhile. Suddenly he said he was leaving, and the next day I learned the domestic problem had been peaceably settled.

Asa Daklugie

Geronimo's nephew, eighty-year-old Asa Daklugie, was a towering old man, still well over six feet tall when I first saw him at Whitetail. Until I read Eve Ball's account of his early life and experiences, I never realized why he rarely smiled and talked so little. When he was still an impressionable child, before the surrender, he saw his mother and several siblings brutally killed by soldiers. Two of his brothers were carried off by Mexicans and probably enslaved. Neither Asa nor anyone else ever saw them again.

During the early prisoner-of-war years Asa attended Carlisle School, entering on December 8, 1886. On November 7, 1895, he left the school and traveled to Fort Sill to join his family. In 1898 he married his childhood sweetheart, Ramona Chihuahua, a former classmate at Carlisle and the daughter of Chief Chihuahua. They celebrated their fiftieth wedding anniversary in 1948 while I was at Whitetail, but I was not invited to attend. As a matter of fact, he spoke only a few words to me during the entire two years I taught at Whitetail. "Hello, teacher," were the friendliest.

Asa's dislike, even hatred, of white people lasted his entire life. He talked to Eve Ball only because she convinced him that it was important to record his tribe's history in writing from the Apache point of view, and he knew that she could help him tell his people's side of the story.

At the end of the period of incarceration, Daklugie was one of the leaders of the group that decided to move to New Mexico. He was a prominent spokesman for the people there until his death in 1955. Most of what I know about Asa I learned from reading Eve Ball's book, *Indeh: An Apache Odyssey*. Their discussions together and interviews over a twenty-year period produced a book that gives readers a remarkable look inside Apache culture.

Robert Geronimo told me that Asa helped persuade Geronimo to surrender, a belief that is in conflict with Ball's information. Eve Ball stated Asa did not become a scout until after he became a prisoner, and her conclusion makes more sense to me because noted genealogy authority Gillett Griswold recorded that Asa was born in 1872.[8] If this information is correct, Asa would have been fourteen years old at the time of the negotiations that led to the band's final surrender in 1886. I very much doubt that Geronimo, in that delicate situation, would have paid close attention to the words of a teenager, even someone considered to be his own nephew. Still, the oral tradition of a people should not be discounted, and it is possible that young Asa contributed in some way to the discussions leading to the capitulation. He was, after all, the son of Geronimo's beloved cousin Ishton.

After Ramona died (hers was the only funeral that I attended at Whitetail, and the only one, I understand, where the usually unemotional Chiricahuas actually wept), I seldom saw Asa anymore at Whitetail. Someone told me that he moved and was living with a daughter some distance away. Later I learned that Asa and Ramona's home had received a traditional cleansing but had not been burned, as it would have been in the old days, because the government had banned this time-honored practice. I wondered why Asa did not want to be at Whitetail near his daughter Maude at such a painful time. Once I forgot my manners and asked Robert what was going on, but he only winced and changed the subject, as if there was some cloud over Ramona's death. Only retrospectively did I become aware of the Chiricahua taboo against speaking of the dead, and then I observed it as well. Mentioning the name of a deceased individual reminds relatives of death, and then they feel sad, which, of course, is something not to cause. If it is absolutely necessary to bring up the name of a dead person in conversation, there are several polite ways to do so. For example, you might say, "that fellow who lived out in the woods and used to be the uncle of so-and-so" or "that woman who was always happy and told so many jokes."

Charles Istee

Charles Istee was the only child of Chief Victorio and his wife (herself the daughter of Mangas Coloradas, another famous Apache leader) to survive the Apache wars and become a prisoner of war. Eight years old at the time his father was killed in October, 1880, he was fourteen at the final surrender. Charlie left the Florida prison site in April, 1887, for Carlisle School, where he remained until early November, 1895. After leaving Carlisle he went to Fort Sill and lived among his friends and relatives. Charlie met and later married later Dora Chaenedee, another prisoner of war, and fathered one daughter, who died at Fort Sill. A son, Evans, was born in 1913 soon after the newly freed family established a homesite on a sloping hill at Whitetail. One of their close neighbors was the former warrior known as Dahteste.

Charlie (very few people called him "Charles") was a short, wiry man close to eighty years old when I first knew him. Several of the Chiricahua men looked very old to me, and Charlie was one of them. His face was lined like a road map, and his wrinkles were especially pronounced when he sat on my stoop and, grinning, spun tales of long ago. I was amazed by his memory. He seemed to know how many Apache scouts had gone out on a certain foray and how many troops had met them, although he never mentioned how many had died in the encounter. When he described the battles Charlie actually seemed to relive the old times. His whole countenance brightened. It was almost as if he were all alone, talking to himself. He looked past me or through me back into history to a bygone time that very few Americans, whatever their background, can recall. With his permission I took a photo of him after one of these reminiscences. He was sitting on the teacherage steps, in the same spot where Robert Geronimo once sat to be photographed.

Charlie never tired of telling me about his father and his maternal grandfather. It was certainly a lineage to cherish. Both men were powerful leaders and warriors of great integrity and character. They were respected by all who knew them, by friend and foe alike. Charlie once mentioned that when he was about eight years old, his father was killed. He was careful to lay all the blame on the Mexicans, whose fault it was, according to history.

Charlie told me that the Apaches loved nothing more than to put one over on the "white eyes," and he would joke about the U.S. cavalry, but never said anything bitter about them. As he told the stories, he almost seemed to be analyzing a game of chess. Charlie recounted in fair detail an adventure that took place when he was a youthful member of a raiding party, laughing at how easy it was for them to trap the cavalry. Two or three of the Warm Springs band kept a lookout for soldiers. When they spotted a small troop, they signaled the others to get ready. A few decoys rode out on a ledge so that the soldiers could hardly miss seeing them. As soon as they had been spotted by the troops, they pretended to run away, staying just far enough ahead to be seen, but not close enough to be caught.

According to plan, the decoys rode into a box canyon from which there was no exit. The other members of the band were waiting on the cliffs above with ropes, which they lowered to the decoys. The decoys grabbed the ropes and were pulled up to safety. When the soldiers came inside the box canyon searching for the vanished Apaches, the men above rained down rocks to block the entrance to the canyon, then picked off the helpless soldiers trapped below, often by shooting the horses from beneath them. As the soldiers frantically scurried for their lives, the amused Apaches carefully and deliberately took aim and shot at their leisure. Charlie would slap his thigh, rocking back and forth with laughter, as he recalled such exploits. I heard no tales about fights the Apaches lost.

He also told me that his father's men could lie for hours so still on the ground that the soldiers could pass right by on foot and not even see them. "You don't look at them and they don't see you," he said. And often he avoided looking me in the eye when he told these stories, which might have been an observance of Apache etiquette. Charlie could not comprehend the white men's stupidity in sending military leaders into the field who were not acquainted with Indian ways—and, he would say, perhaps not even interested because they thought they had learned everything there was to know about war at West Point. Officers who became seasoned fighters and a real threat to the Apaches were invariably replaced by green officers, too proud or too arrogant to listen to the experienced enlisted men or even to learn from outgoing officers. A few wily old generals got smart enough to use Indian scouts to track down other Indians, Charlie remembered, but the government did not trust any Indians. The white soldiers paid a heavy price in blood for their condescending attitudes, he concluded, smiling at his memories.

He mentioned several times seeing the soldiers jumping and splashing in water after not finding any for days. Charlie had no admiration for the military men for enjoying the opportunity to bathe. Instead, he commented sarcastically that, unlike the Apaches, the troopers obviously were unaccustomed to going without water for days.

Another military procedure that caught Charlie's fancy was the drilling performed by the troops. He equated this activity with the Apache war dance, saying that when the Apaches did such exercises, they meant business. He also laughed at the soldiers for following leaders they did not respect. And he could not understand the army's strategy of having the officers stand on mountain tops with field glasses while their men went into battle. Apache warriors followed the leaders they respected into a fight, not the other way around.

When Charlie finished telling his tales of the Apache wars, always including some facial expressions of his disdain for the way the U.S. Army conducted its business, he would look at me to get my reaction. Usually I was quiet or would only nod in agreement. Then he would throw back his head and laugh, laugh, laugh. In a reflective moment now, by listening carefully, I can almost hear him. Sometimes his recitations made me wonder who really had won the Indian wars. Could that have been what he wanted?

One day when Charlie was sitting on my porch, he looked down at the grass growing around the house. Suddenly he pointed to a plant and said it would make good medicine. When I encouraged him to take it he refused, saying that it was not ready yet. He said it could heal bites, but he added no details. He also noted that some of the men and women at Whitetail could find a cure for almost anything right there and that they really had no need for a doctor. Come to think of it, I remember watching some of the elders pull up the root of what I thought was a weed and then eat it after they rubbed off the soil with their fingers.

One thing I think Charlie would ruefully appreciate is an embarrassing story told about him, but I think I owe him one. Dorcie Kazhe, my cook, told me about the time when Charlie and his wife, Dora, took their old truck down the mountain to do some shopping in Mescalero. With a load of groceries, they began to make their way back along the highway to the turnoff to Whitetail. Just as they reached the turnoff, the truck stalled. Charlie told Dora he thought it would take both of them to get it going, and she dutifully walked around to the back of the vehicle to join her husband in pushing. Charlie's instructions were clear, according to Dorcie. "When we get it started," he said, "we'll both run around and jump in and drive on." Easy enough, but ... Charlie drove off and forgot Dora. When he got back to Whitetail, somebody asked where his wife was. "Oh, my!," Charlie exclaimed. "I forgot her back on the highway." Just about then the cow camp truck came along, and Dora was in it, having hitched a ride shortly after Charlie pulled away.

More idle chatter about Charlie had to do with his homelife with Dora, whom he called his "old lady." He complained about her being a little bossy at times. Charlie was out well after dark one night, and that made Dora angry, so the story goes. Knowing her husband was a creature of habit, in his absence she moved the living room furniture. When he crept in, he automatically sat where the couch had been and promptly fell on his rear end. Dora, lying awake in bed, had to hide her giggles in the pillow.

The stories I heard about Charlie and Dora Istee could fill a small book. Dorcie remembered helping Dora can some meat once and telling her to leave a little room at the top of the jar for expansion. Dora said,

"Nah, nah, nah. That's the white man's way. We're going to do it our way and fill the meat right up to the top and put the lids on." They were in the next room a short time later when the explosions began. The tops blew off, and the white man had nothing to do with it.

Charlie, Hugh Chee, and other elders were quite concerned about the next generation. They decried the passing of the old ways. Few of the younger Apaches were good hunters, they thought, and most could not shoot as well as the older folks. Some of the older men still preferred bow and arrow hunting to shooting. An arrow was better than a gun, I remember someone said, because if you missed, the game stayed put, and you could get in another shot. Turkeys, for example, flew only once. Then they had to walk around a while to get enough energy to fly again. Meanwhile, an Apache could shoot another arrow because the birds had not been scared off by the sound of gunfire. The men also felt that an arrow made a better kill. Shotguns filled the bird with pellets and sometimes, after cooking, you might bite down on one and break a tooth. An arrow, on the other hand, was clean and left nothing behind when it was pulled out.

I enjoyed Charlie's stories, but there was much he left unsaid. Like most of the others, he never talked about the years of imprisonment. Everyone's stories usually skipped from the days of freedom to the days at Whitetail. Through the years, whenever I have remembered Charlie, the Apache version of history has filled my imagination and dozens of questions have popped into my mind. What has kept people from learning the full story? History is written by the victors, I know, but why not depict the view of the Chiricahuas? I am still deeply troubled by it all.

Evans Istee

Charlie Istee's son, Evans, was always very friendly, and he seemed to be a very nice person. So I was puzzled one afternoon after school was dismissed when I saw his wife walking up the road toward the teacherage. She stopped me in the driveway, saying she needed to speak with me right away. We sat outside on the screened porch and she confided her problem: she was afraid that Evans was going to shoot her if she went back home. Although she looked very serious, she appeared to be calm, but then I rarely saw any Chiricahua really excited. (Once, in my two years at Whitetail, a terrified Apache cowboy came rushing in to tell me that there was a monster scaring the cattle out on the range. It turned out to be a buffalo; the cowboy had never seen one before. No one knew how it got there.) Mrs. Istee could offer no motive for Evans's anger, so the first thing that came to my mind was alcohol. But Evans was neither a drinker nor a violent man. I grabbed the receiver on the old wooden wall phone and cranked for the agency operator but got no answer. Then I started to panic. "You can stay here," I offered, motioning to the living room. "I'll send for the sheriff when someone is back at the switchboard." "No," she answered. "Can't stay here. Have to go home now." She left the porch and started walking toward their cottage, which was across the road from Charlie's place, about a mile west of the school. "Wait," I called. "I'll go with you."

I jumped in the pickup truck and loaded her aboard. Even though resolving domestic disputes was not part of my job, I had to make sure everything was all right. As the truck bumped along the road, I prayed that Evans would not be there. I had absolutely no idea what I would do if there was a confrontation. Their four-room home looked empty when we walked in, but I heard footsteps in one of the other rooms. It was Evans, friendly enough at first. "Hey, teacher," he said. "What's the trouble?" He was wearing an odd, quizzical expression. "Your wife said you threatened to shoot her," I growled, trying to look bold and fearless. Evans turned to his wife. "What did you say that for?" he asked, his face clouding over with anger. Then, looking at me, he said, "She's a crazy woman. She made it all up. I got no guns here." Taking a deep breath, I replied, "Could I just have a look around?" Evans was cooperative. "Nothing's here. See for yourself."

I made a brief search through the small rooms and came back into the corner of the living room. Evans stood squarely in front of the one closet, his feet planted like tree trunks on the wooden floor. "See, what did I tell you? She's a crazy woman, just trying to make trouble." His voice was firm. I looked past him at the closet door, and he backed up to it, protecting it. "Could I look in there?" I asked. Grudgingly, he stepped aside. Inside the closet was an arsenal of knives and guns of all descriptions. I felt perspiration form on my forehead. No one spoke. I knew they were both waiting for me to say something. I did. "Now I know you've got guns. Just make sure nothing happens to your wife or I'll be back."

Imitating John Wayne, but not having a weapon like he did for security, I swaggered back to the pickup truck and drove off. I had just faced down a Chiricahua Apache, and sweat beaded my brow. Fortunately for me, and for Evans's wife, he took me seriously and nothing happened to her—then. Years later, though, long after I had left the reservation, Evans decided he had finally had enough of whatever he believed she did. He took one of those knives and slit her throat, ear to ear. She bled to death, and he went to prison for murder.

No one would go near his place for a long time after that. Evans's mother, Dora, told Dorcie Kazhe that the ghost of Evans' wife still lived in the house. Dora, herself, had heard the dead woman call "woo, woo, woo" one night. So scared was Dora that she jumped behind a tree stump to hide. But Dorcie thought maybe it was her kids, Peter and Lynette, who scared poor Dora. In fact, the children confessed some time later that they were the ones who called "woo, woo, woo" out into the darkness to deliberately frighten poor Dora Istee.[9]

Hugh Chee

Hugh Chee, a nephew of Cochise, was seventy-six years old when he felt comfortable enough with me to tell me some of the unforgettable events in his life. He said he had been a child when the Apaches surrendered and still remembered some of the great warriors like Geronimo, Chihuahua, Nana, and Loco. He recalled being chased more than once by the U.S. cavalry and remembered one particularly harrowing pursuit. When his family was finally safe and could breathe easier, they looked around to find that his mother and young sister were not there. Hugh concluded that they must have been killed because he never saw them again.

Hugh was one of the children taken away from their families during the Apaches' first months of imprisonment at Fort Marion in St. Augustine, Florida. Along with at least one hundred other Chiricahua youngsters, Hugh was sent to Carlisle School to learn the white man's ways. He did well there but never forgot his own customs and his heritage. Hugh was very proud of having survived the imprisonment years, and he always denied being bitter, just grateful that the experience had not destroyed him.

This gentleman was a very religious fellow and continued the spirituality of his ancestors. He said that he prayed from the time he got up until he went to bed, but especially after hunting or planting at Whitetail. He lamented that the young ones often never bothered to pray, implying in his way that they were following the white man's path. Knowing how close he felt to the unseen world, I was not surprised when Hugh mumbled something about a supernatural experience, but he told it in the Apache way, cloaked in obscure language, and I had a hard time catching the point. When Hugh mentioned passing over into another world and seeing some long-dead friends and then coming back, I could not tell whether he was talking about his own experience, or something he had heard from someone else, or whether he was repeating a tribal legend. He used the term "happy hunting ground" as though trying to translate it so that I would understand. Maybe he assumed that all white people called the afterworld by that term. The place Hugh described was not like the Christian idea of heaven or hell. He said that a great Apache had once brought back some of the old chiefs from their graves, and many saw them. Hugh himself never saw them, but he thought some of those still living at Whitetail (whom he neglected to name, and I had learned enough not to ask) remembered the incident.

Another one of our conversations was about Chiricahua polygamy. Hugh said he once had four wives at the same time. The government opposed the practice but never forced him to give any up. I remember asking him, almost jokingly, if the women got along with each other. He said that they appreciated having others to share the work and the baby-sitting. He admitted that he had a favorite, but said that he treated them all the same. One of his wives was the former wife of his deceased brother. When we talked about it, he asked, "Who else would take care of my brother's wife?"

His commendable concern about his dead brother's wife and his actions in marrying her no doubt had their roots in the long-standing Chiricahua custom called by anthropologists the "levirate." This tradition prescribes that when a married man dies, his widow belongs to his family, particularly to his brothers and male cousins. Any of these men can marry her, but if none chooses to do so within a reasonable period of time, or if there are no male members of the family suitable for marriage, the widow is free to wed others. Until she does so, however, she is directly responsible to her dead husband's family and owes them courtesy and obedience. If intrafamilial marriage does occur, the widow's brother-in-law becomes the step-father of her children, thus permitting continuity to occur and avoiding an abrupt disruption of family life. This custom, although now impossible to trace back to its origin, allowed for a sequence of relationships that provided uninterrupted stability to the core of Chiricahua life—the family.

Hugh told me it was customary among free Chiricahua men to have more than one wife, and when that occurred, each family occupied different living quarters. There was no limit to the number of wives a Chiricahua could have; wealthy men sometimes had three or even more, but if such cases did occur, they were rare. The practice may have been especially encouraged in the latter days of freedom because so many men had fallen in battle that the women greatly outnumbered them.

Cultural provisions were also in place in case a married woman died and left children. They were taken and cared for by a sister or female cousin of their dead mother. The woman who elected to care for the children could become the widower's next wife (anthropologically called the "sororate"). If the woman had no female relatives, her husband became free to marry any other woman after receiving permission from his in-laws and giving them gifts.

Under certain circumstances, a Chiricahua man took a wife by doing nothing more than seeing an attractive woman and deciding to be with her. For example, Geronimo liked the looks of Ih-tedda, so during one of his breakouts from the San Carlos Reservation he took her along. Another example concerns a number of Mexican women washing clothes in a stream. Geronimo rode by, stopped, looked, and forced one of the women to ride with him; she became his Mexican wife, or so the story goes.

However, not all relationships between Apache men and women began so abruptly. Flirting occurred, courtship (often timid) always proceeded, and a serious young man first discussed marrying with his parents and their siblings. Along with giving their consent, one of these relatives volunteered to approach the young woman's family to obtain their permission. But if the fellow's family thought his judgment was faulty, regardless of any emotional involvement, he had to look elsewhere. If all were in agreement, the family accumulated presents, often horses, saddles, and guns to present to the future bride's relatives, usually by the fellow's father. In conversation accompanying the presents, the father first extolled his son's virtues and the quality of the gifts and then requested the marriage. Once again agreement became necessary, this time by the other family. After reaching consensus, the members of both families appeared at the young woman's camp, feasting and dancing occurred, and then everyone watched the young couple walk off into a dwelling specifically built for them by the bride's female relatives. Marriage had then occurred. Later, simultaneous marriage with other women did not always require the involvement of parents and families.

Polygamy was not permitted when the Apaches were released from prison and moved to Mescalero in 1913. According to Hugh, at that time the men who had had more than one wife were allowed to continue supporting them, but they could never add any more wives. Some men, including Hugh, who had several spouses, joined the Catholic Church at Mescalero because the priest made no issue of their marital status. Perhaps the priest was more sympathetic to the events that impacted the Chiricahuas in the past, including the chronic and fatal illnesses suffered while the people were incarcerated.

Our conversations also included more mundane topics such as alarm clocks. I recall that I loaned Hugh my extra clock after he remarked that his was broken. I was surprised that any Apache cared what time it was at Whitetail, but frankly, I was glad to be rid of the darn thing because it had ticked so loudly that it kept me awake. I bought another one to take its place but kept the noisy one, just in case. After Hugh had the clock for a while, someone told me that I needed to retrieve it as soon as possible because Hugh was going to die the next day. If I failed to reclaim my property, it would be buried with him, according to Chiricahua Apache tradition. The individual who told me that Hugh was going to die said he knew it because the coyotes had howled, and whenever that happened, someone died. I listened carefully, and never questioned how he knew it would be Hugh because he would not have told me anyway. Then I walked on over to Hugh's house. My friend was sitting comfortably on his porch and, as far as I could see, he was not suffering from any malady whatsoever. We sat together and had a long, rambling chat. When I rose to leave, he casually handed me my clock, saying he had no further need of it anymore. He died that night and was buried in a cemetery, unlike many of his ancestors.

In the high southwestern desert of Arizona, New Mexico, and northern Mexico—Apache country of old—it was often futile to try to open a gravesite in sandy soil that ordinarily was crammed full of various-sized rocks and criss-crossing mazes of thick tree and shrub roots. The Apaches devised alternative means of respectfully disposing of a person's remains. History notes that when Chief Cochise died on June 8, 1874, his interment took place somewhere in the Chiricahua mountain range of eastern Arizona, a wild land, full of hidden places. At the time of his demise the Chiricahuas were at peace, giving his loved ones opportunity to properly prepare his body. Assuming traditional practices were followed, soon after death his wife or his sister washed, groomed, and dressed him in head feathers and war garments, then bathed themselves in the smoke of the sage plant, and, before sleeping that night, placed ashes near their beds as a precautionary measure against harm. Chiricahuas had strong taboos against touching dead bodies, so specific cultural activities, such as the protective use of ashes, were designed to purify those who were obliged to handle corpses. The women undoubtedly took great care in preparing Cochise's body for the four-day journey to the next world, for Chiricahuas believed that the physical condition of the body at death was the way the deceased would travel through eternity. The next day they placed Cochise on his favorite horse and guided the mount through the rocks and chasms of the Apache stronghold to a rough and lonely place where there was a deep fissure in the cliff. The horse was killed and dropped into the depths, as was the leader's favorite dog. Cochise's gun was thrown in and then the chief was lowered with ropes into the gorge. Family members later destroyed his belongings by fire.

Chiricahua warriors killed in battle often did not have the blessings of customary funeral rites. Mimbres Apache chief Mangas Coloradas, for example, was captured by a mountain man who turned him over to military authorities. On the night of January 13, 1863, guards tortured the chief until he struggled and gave them an excuse for shooting him. Some time later his head was severed from his body and the skull boiled. Still today, its whereabouts remain a mystery.

Warm Springs Apache chief Victorio died during a fight with Mexican troops at Tres Castillos, Mexico. While it is said that his body was tended by surviving members of his band, it is improbable that the dangerous situation would have permitted time to conduct ancient burial rites.

Such was also the case with Geronimo's first family. When the young warrior returned to camp from a trading expedition to Janos, Mexico, in the 1850s, he found that his mother, wife, three children, and many others, left behind earlier, were now dead, killed by Mexican troops. Geronimo turned from the bloody scene and, following instructions from the chief, went immediately to Arizona, leaving the dead upon the field. Before Geronimo died from pneumonia in February, 1909, he had embraced Christianity on and off, enabling Rev. Leonard Legters, the Dutch Reformed Church minister at Fort Sill, Oklahoma, to conduct the service. It is obvious that during the thirty-five-year interim since Cochise had been traditionally buried, the Christian influence had replaced the older Apache customs, at least for some. Nonetheless, the death practices of a former time still lived in the memories of certain venerable Apaches.

The old-timers like Hugh Chee impressed me with their recollections of long ago. I often wondered if they made up the stories, or at least embellished them, because there was so much detail. Years later, however, when I studied the Old Testament in seminary, I was deeply affected by the way the scripture was passed down by memory from generation to generation. Reliance on recollections is a method so foreign to us in this computer age that it is hard to believe that memory was a sufficient record for millennia, even in all the diverse cultures of the world.

Jasper Kanseah, Sr., and His Family

Jasper Kanseah, Sr., was Geronimo's nephew and was his youngest apprentice warrior when Geronimo surrendered in 1886. Born in 1873, Kanseah lived through nearly three decades of imprisonment, including the hard school years in Carlisle.[10] At the time of the surrender he was being trained by Yah-no-sha, a great warrior, and was serving as his horse holder. According to Chiricahua tradition, Kanseah had been prepared all of his young life to become a warrior. During peaceful times, as a small boy he played among the rocks and pines with other children, leaping from boulder to boulder, running, crawling. He whittled toys, fashioned bows and arrows out of soft wood, and hunted wild fruits and nuts. As he got older, he rose before sunrise, bathed in a creek even when ice covered the water, and raced up the side of a mountain carrying water in his mouth. He shot small game and was taught how to hide, track, map the terrain, and find his way back to camp. In Geronimo's tightly organized band, youngsters all had assigned duties. Caring for the horses was an important job in that equestrian society, and the boys were expected to perform their duties conscientiously and well. Naturally, all that ended abruptly with the surrender.

Jasper Kanseah, Sr., the young horse holder, came to Mescalero as an adult in 1913 with the other freed Chiricahua Apache prisoners of war. His first wife, whom he married while incarcerated, was called Tah-de-cloey-eh. They had one child, Flora, who died a prisoner, as did Tah-de-cloey-eh, in 1899. Jasper then married Lucy Gon-altsis and they had three children, also born into captivity: Jasper, Jr., Jean, and Rola. Several other children were born to them at Whitetail after the release. Always interested in the youngsters, Jasper liked to drop by the school every now and then to see how his grandchildren were doing. At the same time he made certain that all the kids were behaving. When they saw him they were as good as gold.

As a matter of fact, they always showed me respect when parents or grandparents were around. But when we were alone they became like all other children, rowdy, boisterous, and sometimes downright disrespectful. Although Jasper Kanseah, Sr., usually kept very much to himself, I remember that one winter his pipes froze, and he came to the school for water. How he must have longed for the days of freedom in the desert climates of Arizona and New Mexico, where there was no such thing as a winter cold enough to cause plumbing problems, or any plumbing to worry about, for that matter. Nonetheless, the old fellow made the best of his life as a prisoner of war, rearing a family and living each day to the fullest. He died at Whitetail in 1959.[11]

Jasper Kanseah, Jr., was born at Fort Sill in 1908. When I knew him he was about forty years old, a proud-looking, serene man with slightly graying hair, about average height and barrel-chested, with the typical round Apache face. He was a good-natured man and the most dependable bus driver I had. He spoke slowly and deliberately, perhaps because he always seemed short of breath.

Jasper, Jr.'s son Berle was the brightest of the students. As Berle always finished his schoolwork before the others, I would send him to teach the second or third grades while I went on to the fourth or fifth grades. It was a real juggling act, and by recess I was usually exhausted, but I never figured out a better way of managing my work.

Hugh Coonie

Hugh Coonie was born in the Alabama prison camp in 1893 to William and Beteir Coonie. His father had been called Kuni when he rode as a scout with Chatto during the Apache campaigns of the 1880s. It is probable that Hugh and his sister, Eliza, two years older, were the only children of this marriage.

After Beteir's death at Fort Sill, Kuni married Dahteste, a sister of Apache chief Chihuahua's wife. No children were born to this marriage, but the couple reared Hugh and Eliza at Mescalero.[12] Dahteste was known affectionately by everyone as "Old Lady Coonie," and I have already described how she rode her burro up and down the dirt road in front of the school and refused to speak a word of English. As a white man, even though I was a member of the community and friendly with many Chiricahuas, I was an example to her of everything she and her people had suffered. Although she undoubtedly was aware of my presence, she never in any way acknowledged my existence. The few times I came face to face with her, she looked right through me.

In the old days Dahteste had been one of the handful of Apache women who accompanied the men as equals in raiding parties. The Chiricahuas had no quota system prescribing that a certain number of women could be warriors, nor did they have any laws prohibiting the practice. The need in most Apache bands, however, was for women to perform the traditional female roles and for men to serve as warriors and hunters, each sex fulfilling its roles according to custom. Only an exceptional woman would have been the equal to an Apache man in terms of courage and brutality. No doubt Dahteste was that, but she also performed the tasks given to all Apache women to do.

Years later, at Whitetail she opened her home to stray dogs. Her kindness toward these homeless animals was so well known that the tribal store's butcher saved all the excess bones for her dogs.

Dahteste's stepson, Hugh Coonie, was a great salesman. His first attempt with me was to try to sell me his fiddle for twenty dollars. I was taken aback because he was a good fiddle player much in demand for some of the community dances that were held at the school. During the transaction, Hugh casually poked his callused finger toward a name inside the instrument's scrollwork. "Some Italian fellow," he mumbled, trying to appear offhand. I looked inside and saw the inscription "Fabrica Antonio Stradivari." Obviously, Hugh wanted me to believe he was selling the genuine article. I surprised him by pointing out that if the name were genuine, he could get thousands of dollars for the violin, not a paltry twenty. Undeterred, he tried even harder, but since I had never played the violin and had no incentive to learn, he finally conceded defeat.

Hugh's next attempt at salesmanship also failed. He tried to convince me to buy some special Apache hair tonic that was guaranteed to keep me from growing bald. "You never saw a bald Indian!" he argued.[13] The tonic, he said, was an age-old secret formula of cactus juice known to Indians alone, and he offered it to me for the low price of twenty-five dollars per bottle. I refused. (I should also note, however, that there hasn't been a bald-headed Ove for many generations.)

At last, though, Hugh sold me something—a horse. Marmaduke cost me twenty dollars, twenty-five with his saddle included. I thought it was a great bargain. Only later did I learn from Hugh's son, Leroy, that I had been stung. Leroy said the horse was almost twenty years old and told me that he would have broken a young, spirited Indian pony for me for only five dollars. But I had never ridden before, and I was just as happy to have a lazy old horse.

The first problem I discovered about Marmaduke was that I could hardly get him to move once I had saddled and mounted him. After one of the Apache men finally told me that Marmaduke had been owned by a cowboy who sang to him, I always led off with a ballad about the range. Sure enough, he shifted into low and started plodding along. When I quit singing, Marmaduke quit walking and rotated his ears around in my direction like radar antennae until I began again. I had a very small repertoire, and I had a great deal of trouble filling out any but the shortest trips. My voice also let me down regularly, often before we reached our destination.

On the way home, though, Marmaduke always came to life and took off with a clatter. I had to use all my limited horsemanship skills to restrain him and keep myself from sprawling in the gravel. Hugh suggested that I carry a bag of oats so I could feed Marmaduke at the other end of the line. Once the horse discovered that there were oats at both ends of the trip, I had no more trouble.

When I left Whitetail, I sold Marmaduke to a kiddies' pony stable in Ruidoso because he was so gentle. I felt secure that my old friend was in good hands. The stable paid me twenty dollars for him, and I returned the saddle to Hugh.

Solon Sombrero

Solon was the grandson of a brave Mescalero chief called Natzili, whose son killed a Mexican man for a magnificent saddle, bridle, silver bit, and spurs, and a sombrero that was adorned with four pounds of silver, thus gaining for himself the name Sombrero.[14] On his deathbed Sombrero called his young son, Solon, to his side and passed on the treasures to him. Solon and his mother kept them in a buckskin bag that hung outside the entrance to their tipi, a custom with roots in the days when the Apaches might come under attack at any time. A warrior called to answer an attack would first make certain that his family was able to get away; then he would mount his horse; and, finally, as he hurriedly left camp, he would grab the buckskin bags hanging over the tipi's entranceway. The bags were always safe on the outside of the living quarters; there never was any danger of theft among Apaches.

Solon finished six years of education on the reservation and was then sent away to Albuquerque, where he became a good student and came under the influence of missionaries for the Dutch Reformed Church. He became an interpreter for the missionaries and later was influential in establishing a minister of the Dutch Reformed Church in Mescalero. Solon Sombrero married a daughter of Chief Peso, and the couple reared a fine family on the reservation.

This gentleman was a true orator, and his long talks on the early days were legendary. (Maybe because they never seemed to end.) When he was lecturing, his eyes would become glassy, and he would tilt his head back slightly and begin what reminded me of a chant. Portions of tales of the old times made it through clearly, but some parts disappeared in a string of moralisms, platitudes, and clichés. Solon's sentences, like Saint Paul's, sometimes got lost trying to find their way out of paragraphs. Everyone loved him, of course, for good reasons, and gave him ample respect and plenty of opportunities to speak.

Looking back after all these years, I can see that all the Apaches' speeches, not just his, had several things in common. First, the speeches seemed to have no identifiable beginning. They just took off like birds flushed from their nests, the words coming from nowhere and pelting down like hailstones. Second, the speaker often had no idea where his talk was going. He seemed to run along behind it, never quite catching up with his words. Third, no speaker seemed to have any idea how to stop. There would be pauses, seemingly excellent places to call a halt to the procession, but no one took advantage of them. Sometimes there would be a long silence, and it would look like the speech was finally over, but a random idea would come from somewhere, and the talk would take off in another direction. Folks would continue speaking until someone interrupted.

Quite a few of the speeches appeared to be for the benefit of members of the Apache community. The orators seemed to be trying to impress everyone else with the importance of the fact that a young, inexperienced newcomer was in charge of educating their youngsters. I was amazed at the length and number of speeches, for I erroneously carried the stereotypical image of the stoic Indian, the man or woman of few words full of meaningful ancient philosophy. Obviously, the originator of that depiction had not based it on the Chiricahua personality.

Arthur Johnson

Arthur Johnson was the bus driver I hired to replace Levi. He was a handsome man who seemed to be a competent mechanic and handyman, and he and his wife lived close to the school. His widowed mother-in-law died, leaving one of her daughters still at home. According to the old way, if the parents of a young girl died before she married, or if her husband died leaving her a widow, the husband of one of her sisters automatically married her so that someone was responsible for her. True to their culture, Arthur and his wife took this pleasant-looking young woman into their house to live with them. No one acknowledged openly to me that the old tradition was still followed, but it seemed to me that the understanding was still the same. Arthur, however, was careful not to refer to his sister-in-law as his wife. Bigamy, as the white society defines it, had been outlawed among the Chiricahuas.

The arrangement was not without its problems in Arthur's house. From what he told me, there was jealousy between the sisters—to such a degree that it drove him out more than once. Still, this kindly man made it crystal clear to me that it would be unthinkable for him to move his sister-in-law out.

Before his mother-in-law died, Arthur explained another Apache custom to me. A man's mother-in-law, he said, practically owned him from the day of the wedding. She could order him around like a servant, but she had to dictate the directions or convey her wishes through her daughter or others. She could not speak directly to him, not even to ask him to chop wood, hunt meat, or drive her around, although Arthur certainly did those things, and more, for her.

When Arthur drove his mother-in-law to town, or anyplace, for that matter, both had to show strict respect for the taboos concerning a son-in-law and his mother-in-law. Tradition dictated that to show his respect, a son-in-law should never again lay eyes on his mother-in-law after the wedding day. Actually, each was obligated not to look at the other, although the avoidance onus fell on the man. Arthur's mother-in-law always sat in the backseat of the car, regardless of whether or not the front passenger seat was occupied, and a handkerchief or towel was hung behind Arthur's head so that he would not inadvertently look in the rearview mirror and catch a glimpse of her. The prohibition was observed so strictly that it was upheld even in church. In days long past, a rope was strung down the aisle from the front to the back of the reservation's Dutch Reformed mission. Draped over the rope were curtain-like cloths separating families in order to honor the restriction.

Indirect communication was also a traditional part of the husband-wife relationship. A wife, in the old days, rarely used the familiar form of direct address when speaking to her husband. For example, she would stand in front of him and ask, "Will the man who is my husband please carry out the garbage?" I learned from Hugh Chee that the reverse was also true. A man would ask, "Will the woman who is my wife please bring me a cup of coffee?" Nonetheless, observing the traditions didn't keep the Apaches from having knock-down, drag-out fights, or from having children.

The husband-wife relations never displayed much affection. In the old days, if a man showed his love for his wife, he was ridiculed by his peers. A Chiricahua wife's duty was only to serve her man, to walk behind him, and to find her pleasures in life by associating with other women. Any exceptions allowed by a husband, e.g., a man eating with his wife, showed other men that he was the Apache cultural equivalent of "henpecked," a very undesirable label in Chiricahua society. On the other hand, women could also receive supernatural power, and these special women were often quite important within the group at large. Their suggestions and recommendations were extremely influential in deciding significant matters pertaining to warfare and to the general well being of the people, especially the children.

Arthur and his wife, Clara, had only preschool-aged children when I lived at Whitetail. I learned from Clara recently that Arthur moved a long time ago to the San Carlos Reservation in southern Arizona and died there as a relatively young man. I was not surprised, for Arthur always seemed to have personal problems that weighed heavily on his mind. Certainly these problems, including the time his wife found him in bed with another woman, could have had an adverse affect on his health.

I recently learned that the *adulterer's* nose could also be sliced for adultery, and often was, usually by someone in the wife's family. My anonymous (at his request) informant added that if that same practice were carried on today, there would be very few Apaches with a whole nose. Fortunately for Arthur, he did not live in those old times.

One day when the school's cook was sick, Arthur and I had to prepare the noon meal for the children. More than ninety percent of the food in the pantry was either canned or powdered, and we took out a big pan and poured in powdered egg, powdered milk, dried meat, and a few other odds and ends to make a tasty, succulent casserole. The kids said it was fit only for pigs and refused to eat it, so Arthur and I, and the wild animals, feasted while the students settled for bread and butter.

Delores Enjady

Long before I arrived, it had been the custom to feed the children lunch at school. Delores Enjady, a nice-looking woman in her late twenties or early thirties, was the cook when I arrived. Delores taught me much about Apache customs. For example, she told me that Apaches never eat liver, but they do eat "mountain oysters," the testicles of a donkey. An age-old taboo prohibits eating bear meat, based on the belief that evil ancestors may return to earth in the form of bears. She said that most Apaches eat fish nowadays, but prior to the imprisonment no one ate anything that swam under water. In the old days, horse meat had been a favorite food. By the time I met the Chiricahuas most of them ate only beef, but Delores recalled being happy to eat horse meat during World War II when it became more available. Mexican food has always been popular among the Chiricahuas, probably because, according to her, the Apaches took so many Mexican women captive that the people grew accustomed to Mexican cuisine. I question that, though.

The dances and movies at the school brought another custom to my attention: women nursing older children. Delores explained that the custom of keeping a child at the mother's breast until almost school age originated in the days when the Chiricahuas were running for their lives. It was often too dangerous to stop and prepare food, so the adults went hungry while children, even up to five and six years old, were nursed by their mothers.

Delores had a daughter, Wynelle, in my fourth-grade class. She was a cute little girl and very quiet, unlike her mother. Once Delores got started talking, it was quite a while before she stopped. Her boys, Zeno and Collins, who were somewhat younger than their sister, were also my pupils. Zeno was quieter than his gabby mother, but Collins was a little chatterbox.

About a month after school started, Delores discovered that she was pregnant. There was a government rule against employing pregnant women, and regulations said that a replacement for her had to be found. Fortunately, the search for another cook took a long time, and Delores, a hard worker and happy to earn her meager wages, was able to keep the job during the first autumn I was at Whitetail.

One day when Delores's pregnancy was near term, the bus driver skipped work, and I took his place. When I stopped to pick up Delores's children, I discovered that she was in early labor. She asked if I would take the kids on to school and then arrange to have another woman care for them afterward. I agreed, expecting that they would be away from her for a few days at least. When she appeared at the school the very next day with the new little one strapped in her cradleboard (some call it a cradle) and asked for her children, I was speechless. But it was the Apache way.

The baby carriers used by the Apache women at Whitetail were made of natural wood cut from the surrounding forest. Rarely, a length of barbed wire might form the frame's foundation. Each cradle had a strong slatted back and a curved top, making it simple and convenient to pick up. The child was laced into the frame in a vertical position; the contraption could be carried on the mother's back, or placed upright in a corner, or even hung from a hook on the wall. When it was time for the child to learn how to walk, he or she was set free, but the child was always placed back in the carrier at the end of the exercise. I never saw an Apache baby crawling, and I wondered if being upright in the cradleboard helped them to walk earlier. It seemed to me that they were up on their feet long before the non-Indian babies I had seen.

Each tribe that used cradleboards crafted them according to traditional styles. The Chiricahuas relied on oak or yucca cactus frames bound by buckskin straps and backed with yucca stalks. The stalks were split in half and laced with buckskin. A crown shaded the baby's head; for a boy, it had four parallel slits, and for a girl it had a full moon or half moon. The buckskin lace tie-ins were placed on the right for a girl, on the left for a boy. Occasionally, small items were hung from the top of the cradleboard to aid in the development of the infant's eyes. These could be feathers, pine cones, a squirrel's tail, arrowheads, beads of all sorts, or any talisman that assured good health and a long life for the child.

In the old days, when an Apache woman rode horseback, she kept her baby strapped on her back in a cradleboard. A leather strap encircled the mother's forehead, and she could balance the carrier on her back by moving her head, even when the horse was at a full gallop. In the 1950s at Whitetail, the women wore the strap around their shoulders—probably a sign of changing times and styles. Eve Ball spoke of seeing a woman on horseback with a cradleboard; the cradleboard fell, but its design and careful construction kept the child inside from being hurt.[15]

An Apache cradleboard was usually made four days or more after the birth of the baby. When Delores came to work with her newborn the day after giving birth, it was obvious that the baby was in a carrier borrowed from his older siblings, but no one ever explained that to me. I did learn, however, that Delores was hanging wash outside when her labor started, and that she went right back out and finished the job after the delivery. In my eyes, this was yet another impressive example of the Apache way.

Living among the Chiricahua Apache people at Whitetail, I never knew what situation would arise or who would cross my path next. Yet, for all the uncertainties and all the strangeness that so often made me uncomfortable, I would not swap those two years on the reservation for all the comforts and securities of another job anywhere else. Nor would I trade what I learned about the Chiricahua Apaches, from their own lips, for anything similar that has occurred in my life since. Without any fanfare at all, those wonderful people changed the direction of my life.

Geronimo as a prisoner of war at Fort Sill, Oklahoma, ca. 1909.
Courtesy H. Henrietta Stockel

Original Bureau of Indian Affairs hand-carved sign for the school. Note feather headdress, characteristic of Plains Indians, not Chiricahua Apaches. Photograph by Rev. Robert S. Ove

Teacherage at Whitetail, Autumn, 1948. Photograph by Rev. Robert S. Ove

Chiricahua girls from the Whitetail class, 1948–49. Photograph by Rev. Robert S. Ove

Whitetail class, 1948–49. Photograph by Henry F. Wershing

Robert Geronimo, son of the warrior, and Ove's close friend at Whitetail, 1950. Photograph by Rev. Robert S. Ove

Levi Hostosewit standing near playground equipment at Whitetail school, ca. 1948. Photograph by Rev. Robert S. Ove

Charles Istee, son of Warm Springs Apache Chief Victorio,
Mescalero Apache Reservation, ca. 1948. Photograph by Rev. Robert S. Ove

Leroy Coonie, grandson of Apache scout Kuni and descendant of Dahteste (Old Lady Coonie), in living room of teacherage, ca. 1950. Photograph by Rev. Robert S. Ove

Myrtis Kanseah, 1950. Photograph by Rev. Robert S. Ove

Jasper Kanseah, Jr., son of Geronimo's nephew and youngest warrior, ca. 1950. Photograph by Rev. Robert S. Ove

Delores Enjady, Ove's first cook at the Whitetail school, ca. 1948. Photograph by Rev. Robert S. Ove

Eugene Chihuahua, son of Chiricahua Chief Chihuahua, his Comanche wife Hernannie, and her three-year-old grandson, Vernon D. Simmons, Mescalero Apache Reservation, 1943. Courtesy Rev. Robert S. Ove

Vernon D. Simmons, 1993. Courtesy Rev. Robert S. Ove

Dorcie and Isaac Kazhe and family, ca. 1948. Photograph by Rev. Robert S. Ove

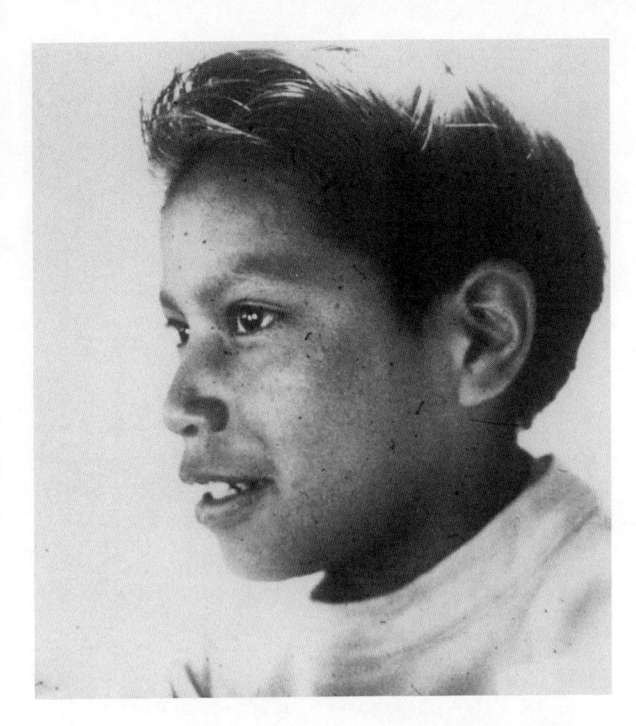

Melvin Kanseah, ca. 1948. Photograph by Rev. Robert S. Ove

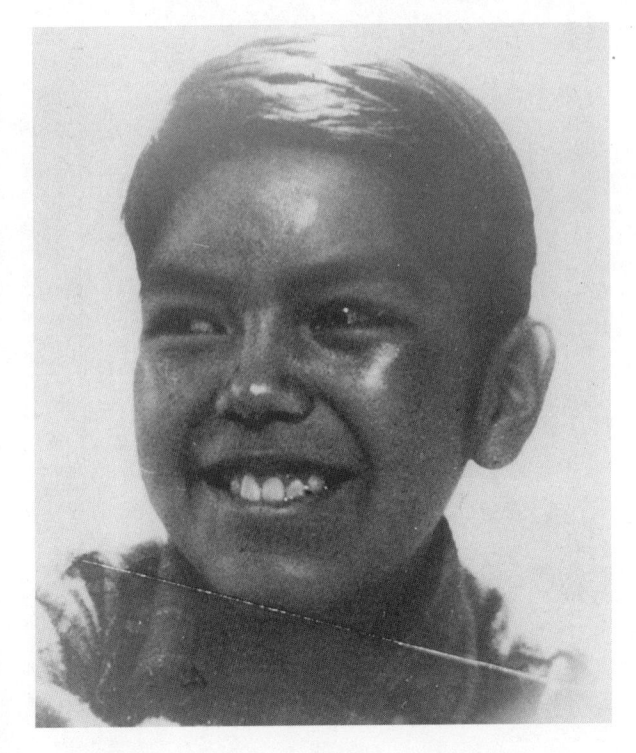

Berle Kanseah, ca. 1948. Photograph by Rev. Robert S. Ove

Wynelle Enjady, ca. 1950. Photograph by Rev. Robert S. Ove

Ulysses Jolsanny, grandson of Ulzanna, Chiricahua warrior and brother of Chief Chihuahua, ca. 1948. Photograph by Rev. Robert S. Ove

Tribal store at Mescalero, ca 1950. Photograph by Rev. Robert S. Ove

Dutch Reformed Church, Mescalero Apache Reservation, under construction, 1950. Photograph by Rev. Robert S. Ove

Charley Smith, medicine man of the Chiricahua Apaches, ca. 1948. Charley was the last Apache to leave Whitetail and move closer to the center of Mescalero. Photograph by Rev. Robert S. Ove

Left to right: *Bernice TenHaken, Maude Daklugie Geronimo (wife of Robert, daughter of Ramona and Asa Daklugie), Vera Shanta (granddaughter of Ramona and Asa Daklugie) modeling ceremonial puberty dresses, ca. 1950. Photograph by Rev. Robert S. Ove*

Ouida Geronimo Miller, granddaughter of the warrior and daughter of Robert, with a descendant. Photograph by Rev. Robert S. Ove

Chapter 5
Religion, Other White Folks, and Chiricahua Apache Justice

My Chiricahua Apache neighbors at Whitetail didn't talk much to me about their traditional religion. When they did respond to my inquiries, they hung their heads and said something like, "Well, some people believe . . ." I assumed at the time that they felt a conflict between their Christian faith and their ancient sacred ways, but I now believe that their reticence came from a deep and well-founded suspicion of what others might think of them. The devastating experience of being literally under the control of military and government officials during the years of imprisonment taught the Chiricahuas to be cautious when answering outsiders' questions. Kathleen Kanseah, in describing some of what it means to be an Apache woman, said candidly, "You have to be careful when you speak, you have to watch what you say to different ones . . . You know who you can talk to . . . My grandmother used to tell me, 'You stand there and you listen and you keep your eyes open but keep your mouth shut.'"[1]

When I innocently asked my Apache friends about their old ways of worship, I seldom got a straight answer. No wonder—most of their rich inheritance of religious rituals had been prohibited during the years of their confinement, and all but two of the old ceremonies were lost during this period. It is not difficult to understand the protectiveness that resulted from that experience.

The traditional rites remaining—the dance of the Mountain Spirits and the puberty ceremony—had their beginnings long ago with White Painted Woman, the revered deity who has control over fertility and is the essence of long life.[2] An ancient legend, one of several Apache creation myths, tells the story of White Painted Woman:

> *There was a time when White Painted woman lived all alone. Longing for children, she slept with the Sun and not long after gave birth to Slayer of Monsters, the foremost culture hero. Four days later, White Painted woman became pregnant by water and gave birth to Born-of-Water (also known as Child-of-the-Water). As Slayer of Monsters and Child-of-the-Water matured, White Painted woman instructed them on how to live. Then they left home and, following her advice, rid the earth of most of its evil. White Painted Woman never became old. When she reached an advanced age, she walked toward the east. After a while, she saw herself coming toward herself. When she came together, there was only one, the young one. Then she was like a young girl all over again. Thus the power of White Painted woman offered the pubescent girl longevity and the physical capabilities of someone perpetually young.*[3]

Lest there be confusion or misunderstanding regarding the identity of the Chiricahuas' supreme deity, however, more than one hundred years ago Geronimo explained the difference between White Painted Woman and *Ussen*, the Almighty. In the beginning, he said, there was a battle between the birds and the beasts, the former wanting light and the latter wanting darkness.[4] After the war was over and the birds were victorious, only a few human beings were alive. One of them was White Painted Woman. Years later she bore a son whom she hid in a cave so that the one beast remaining alive, a dragon, would not find and devour her beloved boy. The disaster almost happened anyway, but the boy finally defeated the dragon with a bow and arrows and was then named Apache. The Giver of Life, *Ussen*, taught the boy how to prepare herbs for medicine, how to hunt, and how to fight. The youngster wore eagle feathers as a sign of justice, wisdom, and power.[5]

White Painted Woman also told the Chiricahuas: "We will have the girls' puberty rite. When the girls first menstruate, you shall have a feast. There shall be songs for the girls. During this feast, the *Gah'e* [masked dancers who represent the sacred mountain spirits] shall dance in front. After that there shall be round dancing and face to face dancing."[6]

While the puberty ceremony and the dance of the Mountain Spirits are the visible manifestations of Chiricahua Apache religion,[7] daily life and religion are hard to separate in the Chiricahua culture. Many aspects of a day's work or play—hunting, gathering herbs, lighting fires, and cooking certain meats, for example—are imbued with spirituality. Each of these functions, and others, may be accompanied by a specific prayer. The shaman's prominent role as spiritual leader, enduring from the days of freedom before 1886, was still part of Apache culture when I lived at Whitetail, as was a very real and deep faith in the God of Scripture.

During my tenure as a teacher there, one of my friends was Charley Smith, Jr., a shaman, or medicine man, who called himself the "witch doctor." Charley's father, Charley Smith, Sr., had been the Chiricahua scout named Ne-do-bilt-yo (meaning "Conceals His Tracks" in the Apache language) before the surrender. After his release, the elder Smith regained his status as a scout and was stationed at Fort Stanton, New Mexico, a few miles from the reservation. According to Eve Ball, the officer who enlisted Ne-do-bilt-yo was unable to either spell his name or pronounce it, so he simply recorded him as Charley Smith. It was a kind of casual disregard that the Chiricahuas experienced again and again. To this day, many descendants of the prisoners have no idea what their family names were before they were given Anglo names.

Charley Smith, Jr., the fellow I knew, had attended the Indian school in Albuquerque. During one summer vacation he met his future wife, the daughter of Muchacho Negro, one of the most formidable men on the reservation. Charley, Jr., served in the army as a scout until he was captured by Mexicans when General John Pershing pursued Pancho Villa into Mexico in 1916. He remained a prisoner of war for about a year. During his military service he was famous for his marksmanship, and he became a scout for Gen. Omar Bradley. Fifty years later, when Bradley visited nearby Fort Bliss, he learned that his former scout Charley was still living and made a special trip to the reservation to see him. "That," Charley told Eve Ball, "was the proudest day of my life."[8]

Charley never said why or how his reputation as a healer got started, and he was not quite sure where he fit into the scheme of things. Nonetheless, he knew instinctively what to do when he saw a patient. An ailing Apache would usually go to the Indian Health Service physician at the public health hospital in Mescalero and take the prescribed therapy or undergo surgery. However, either before or after taking the prescribed treatment, some would also call on Charley's medicine, just in case. He said with a shrug that the people who sought him out must have thought he was doing something to help them. And where both physician and shaman have plied their trade, who can say which brought about the cure? After all, the shaman's treatments have deep religious meaning.[9]

Added to this combination of doctor and healer on the reservation was another element: the Christian churches. The Dutch Reformed Church has been the most significant Protestant influence on the Chiricahuas since John Clum accepted the position of agent at San Carlos on August 8, 1874.[10] A church's impact in such a situation is only as effective as the men and women who represent it. The Dutch Reformed missionaries did an exemplary job among the Chiricahua people, and their translators came to include many of the generation who were born into captivity and at least one middle-aged man, Wheeler Tissnolthos, the son of a former warrior who fought with the Naiche-Geronimo band.

The small Dutch Reformed mission at Whitetail had been built alongside the road on a slight rise just before the bend toward the cow camp. The services, pastored by Reuben TenHaken, were well attended by the Chiricahuas. Yet, despite the obvious devotion of the people, Reuben confessed his doubts to me one day. He worried that the Gospel had penetrated too few hearts, that some people came to church only because a relative pushed them (as when I saw Asa Daklugie there and figured that his wife, Ramona, was the driving force behind his presence). To support his misgivings, Reuben quoted a passage from scriptures: "These people honor me with their lips but their hearts are far from me."

I remember that we discussed the fact that lip service was not unique to the Chiricahuas; it was woefully true among all groups of people. I even admitted to him that I seldom attended Sunday services, even though my parents were devout Lutherans. Reuben's faith was strong, and he responded that if even a tiny seed were planted it would grow, adding that he served at Whitetail for two reasons: the Lord had called him there, not to succeed but to be faithful, and he truly loved the people and wanted them to participate in his enthusiasm for the Gospel.

Pastor TenHaken's hard work was not in vain. The church supported the Ladies' Aid Society, and many of the older Apaches happily attended Sunday services. Regardless of whether the Protestant message registered, they all seemed to enjoy themselves in one way or another. For example, Wheeler Tissnolthos was a superb orator who never missed an opportunity to speak favorably about the teachings of the church, either within its four walls or on other occasions. Unfortunately, he also never missed a chance to continue on and on, long after most of his listeners were exhausted from the effort of hearing him. During the Sunday services, Eugene Chihuahua often raised his magnificent voice in song and praise to *Ussen*, as, occasionally, did Asa Daklugie and Jasper Kanseah, Sr., among others. Eve Ball learned that most of the Chiricahuas saw no conflict between their traditional religion and that of the Old Testament. But, as Asa Daklugie told her, "There are some things in the New Testament that I doubt many Apaches understand—like your queer, three-headed God. And we make no pretense of loving our enemies as you say you do. Have you ever known anybody who really did that?"[11]

The Chiricahuas' lack of resistance to Christian teachings may have been the result of a story told long before recorded time. The oral tradition of a people has preserved a legend that tells that a white man with blond hair and blue eyes and a Bible in his hand would come to visit the Apache people.[12] Although his knowledge of that tale was extremely limited, and consequently so is mine, Pastor TenHaken thought it likely that the story was behind the success of the early missionaries. The whole Apache nation would have been won over, he said, if it hadn't been for the un-Christian activities of certain white people in their dealings with the Indians and with each other. His was referring here to reservation agents affiliated with the Dutch Reformed church, and Reuben was in an excellent position to criticize. He was learned, experienced in the ways of the church, and very popular among the Chiricahua Apaches, as was his wife.

Like many people I met at Whitetail, it seemed there was nothing the TenHakens could not do. One day my wife and I were invited to their house for supper. I appreciated the rare opportunity to spend time with them; they were always so busy. Before dinner was served, the pastor took me out to his barn to demonstrate the art of milking a cow. My subsequent efforts were a total disaster. The cow's tail knocked my hat off, and she stamped her foot so firmly that she scared the wits out of me. I never got near a cow again.

The Dutch Reformed Church was not the only Christian church on the reservation to count Chiricahua Apaches among its parishioners. Saint Joseph's Catholic mission, located far down the mountain near the center of Mescalero, held great sway over many Whitetail residents. Happily, Apache Protestants and Catholics seemed to me to get along very well, as did the clergy. The priest and the pastor were on very friendly terms, and I never sensed any antagonism between any members of my community. Some of the Catholic women would even come to the Dutch Reformed women's group at times, and the Protestant women went to some Catholic events.

The choice between the two denominations seemed to be based more on family differences than on deep theological convictions. When there was a family squabble, one member might go to the "other" church to avoid contact with an offending relative. When the Chiricahuas first arrived at Whitetail in 1913, the Dutch Reformed Church refused to accept polygamous families as members (even though polygamy was a respected Chiricahua tradition dating from their days of freedom), but Saint Joseph's mission, though not approving of these relationships and not blessing them, would look the other way. This was a rather important factor in increasing the size of the Catholic congregation in the early days.

As prisoners of war in Florida, the Apaches were first exposed to Catholicism through the Sisters of the Congregation of Saint Joseph, a group of dedicated nuns who taught the youngest children how to read, write, draw and sing. Although it was not part of the bargain, the nuns taught the adults as well. The children's fathers were so interested in the lessons that they too followed along. Soon they were drawing with crayons and singing simple songs along with the children.[13] It must have been a sight to behold, and one that some of the elders living at Whitetail when I was there might have remembered. But, as I have said, nobody talked about the years of imprisonment, not even about the good things that came from the children's happy affiliation with the nuns of St. Augustine.

Father Marcian Bucher, a jovial and rotund man in his middle to late thirties, was the resident priest in Mescalero in those days, and he became one of my best friends. His portly frame was clothed in official Franciscan garb: a brown cassock that descended almost to his sandals, a white rope sash around his midsection, and a hood that usually languished on his back but could be pulled up to protect his head during inclement weather. He always wore two things on his face: eyeglasses and a huge, friendly smile; when he laughed, which was often, every part of him enjoyed the humor. He looked like the picture of Friar Tuck I have always carried in my mind.

Today, Father Marcian (whom we called "Butch") would be thought of as "laid back." He was easygoing and seemed to have all the time in the world. He often drove to Whitetail in time for supper on the evenings that we had time set aside for religious education at the school. While the meal was being prepared, the chubby Franciscan would circle the sidewalk outside the teacherage (weather permitting), reciting his holy offices from a missal that he pulled from some hidden pocket in his robe. Without thinking, one Friday night back in the days when Catholics were not permitted to eat meat on Fridays, we served roast beef to him. He laughed and declared, "Let's eat!" Then he explained that he could always eat what was set before him, and added that a special dispensation had been granted to

Catholics in the Southwest because when the Spanish conquistadors first arrived, they could find no fish in that dry land.

Both at the dinner table and elsewhere, Butch's conversation was very informal, and he could discourse on an endless variety of subjects, from sports to science. He hardly ever mentioned religion, although we did discuss the ethics and morals of the day. Occasionally he would invite us to Mescalero after Sunday services, and we would take a drive, perhaps finding a restaurant for dinner. Once or twice we dined with him in the manse and the nuns waited on us. I recall a trip we took together to El Paso where we saw the musical *Oklahoma*. Before the show we had time to wander across the international bridge into Juarez, Mexico, where we picked up some cheap booze for Butch and his brother, who came to visit occasionally. During that trip and others we took together, Butch dressed conventionally, often wearing a turtleneck shirt to cover his clericals. As we walked the streets of Juarez, we men were on either side of my wife, but after a lady of the streets accosted Butch and suggested that they "go upstairs together," Butch strolled between my wife and me.

Father Marcian died in 1990 or thereabouts, but we corresponded until then. Father Tom Herbst, a young priest recently at Saint Joseph's mission in Mescalero, remembered him well and had nothing but glowing words for him. Father Tom said that the last time he saw him, Butch was waddling about with the help of a cane, still spouting peppery wit.

Of the Chiricahuas, Robert Geronimo and some others from Whitetail, including the former scout Charles Martine, attended Saint Joseph's. One reason this Roman Catholic church appealed to the Chiricahuas, according to Sister Juanita, a contemporary nun at the modern religious facility, was its practice of permitting the dance of the Mountain Spirits on the grounds.[14] The Apaches were never asked to surrender or compromise their ancient religious heritage in order to belong to Saint Joseph's. As a matter of fact, when the church was being built, the Apaches conducted a ritual inside the unfinished walls.

I recall a night in Whitetail when there was a hushed silence on the mountain—no breath of wind, no movement of trees, not even the chirp of a cricket—and I heard drums in the distance. After pulling on my boots, I walked up the gravel road in the blackness with only my ears and a flashlight to guide me. Finally, ahead and to my left I saw a large bonfire crackling and spitting inside a small opening in the woods. I smelled the delicious aroma of fresh-cut pine burning before I saw a large gathering of

Apaches restlessly moving around the fire. The men jumped first on one foot and then the other in a somewhat crouching stance, while the women did a little sidestep around the circumference. I watched for a while, trying to be unobtrusive, but when they finally noticed me, they were kind enough to invite me over. The men's dance step looked too complicated, so I joined the women and children shuffling on the perimeter of the men's circle. Everybody had a hearty laugh at that; Chiricahua Apache men never, under any circumstances, dance with women. Though I had not the foggiest idea of what I was doing or what it meant, I truly felt part of the community on that night. Although we would always belong to different cultures, there was a good feeling then of mutual acceptance and a growing camaraderie.

One traditional ceremony I witnessed quite frequently was the puberty rite. In the old days youth was prized in a wife, and usually not much time passed between a maiden's puberty rite and her wedding. An early marriage, according to custom, was good for everyone and meant larger families who would carry on the line at a time when many Chiricahuas were being lost to war, starvation, and disease.

Early marriages were no longer the practice in the late 1940s. My cook, Dorcie Kazhe, told me that even if a girl did not marry soon after the ceremony, she often became pregnant almost immediately, sometimes during the week following the ritual. I was told that in the old days a footrace took place near the close of the ceremony when the girl ran out of her tipi and the eligible young men gave chase. Supposedly, the first one to catch her was the future groom. The lucky fellow and the young woman, of necessity, had to be of different family lines and never more closely related than second cousins. In other instances, when a man wanted a wife, he would work out an arrangement with her family. If she concurred, she would feed and water his horse. After that, their honeymoon would be a hunt. Most of the time, I was told, the girl had a choice, but in earlier days the parents could override her objections to a suitor.

Gossip—which young folks were involved with each other, who attended the Protestant and Catholic churches and who didn't, who was taking long trips, was sick or had been involved in an accident of one sort or another—was one of the staples, along with nourishing and not-so-nourishing foods, sold at Juan Baldinado's tribal store in Mescalero. Juan and his wife seemed to be liked by the community. They were honest, friendly, and helpful and they offered the school discounts for quantity.

One day when I had finished loading groceries into one of the school's two vehicles and was resting for a moment beside the old bus, one of the men who usually hung around outside the store spinning yarns with his buddies spotted me and walked over. He showed me a small compression spring and then proceeded to demonstrate an Apache "shave." He held the spring loosely up to his face. When it was almost touching him, a few whiskers had managed to thrust themselves up into the spring. He squeezed it shut and calmly jerked. He showed no emotion, no pain. Then he loosened his grip and let the hairs fall out. He smiled, told me that it was the Indian way of shaving, and encouraged me to follow his example. I took the spring and held it up to my face. Not having used my razor that particular morning, I was a prime candidate for an Apache "shave." Under the man's supervision, I squeezed the spring shut and jerked it, just as he had done. Wow! My cry of pain could be heard all over the reservation. "See how easy it is?" the Apache asked as I handed back the spring and rubbed my sore, red cheek. He walked off and joined the other men in front of the store, and they all moved sedately around the corner. As soon as they disappeared from view, I heard their raucous laughter. They had surely put one over on the "white eyes" teacher.

I usually bought supplies from Juan Baldinado in bulk lots because I never knew when we might be weathered in, during any season of the year. When that happened, the Whitetail residents would come to the teacherage to buy supplies. I usually added a handling and shipping charge to the cost, which I applied toward the purchase of equipment for the little community workshop in the teacherage basement. The people knew where the extra money went, and they never objected. Although I cannot speak for them, they must have preferred to pay me rather than pay Dahteste six dollars to ride into town in the back of her niece's truck to purchase food. Some people walked down the mountain to Mescalero regardless of the weather, but some would grudgingly pay the six dollars—quite a sacrifice in those days—if they could not get a ride back home in the school bus.

We bought case lots of soups, canned vegetables, fruits, soda pop, and junk foods at Juan Baldinado's store to feed the kids at the school. Juan sold everything that was practical, including the Sears catalog, but a few things I would have liked to see—books, art, and photographic supplies—were missing.

When I was in Mescalero to pick up supplies, I usually stopped in to visit with the Hardins (he was the principal at the Mescalero school). There was no restaurant, so lunch was usually on them. Afterward, I made the rounds necessary to meet our needs. For example, if a movie was scheduled, I stopped by the Indian agency to pick up the old Holmes projector. There was no postal delivery to Whitetail, so the only time we got mail was when someone picked it up at Mescalero, and that was usually me. Often I combined these supply runs with a trip to Ruidoso, which had a movie theater, restaurants, and a variety of stores. My wife and I had friends there, and when she went along we often stopped to see them. If those same folks had driven up to Whitetail, we would not visit with them in town again for quite a while.

I recall one occasion when Lonnie Hardin, his wife, Beulah, and their daughter, Melba, planned to have dinner with us at Whitetail.[15] While in transit, Melba somehow opened the back door of the car and fell out. The Hardins had almost reached the teacherage when it happened, so they rushed in for just long enough to make their apologies and then zoomed back down the mountain to the doctor. Melba suffered the physical consequences of that fall for many years.

Without pointing any fingers, I think it is fair to say that nothing that happened in Lonnie's car when he was driving was surprising. On the reservation, his driving style was the stuff of legends. It was he who had driven me up to Whitetail on my first visit. In his big old Lincoln Zephyr he tooled down the rutted dirt roads at breakneck speed, looking his passenger right in the eye when conversing, regardless of the condition of the road or of the speed of the car. Once when we were rounding a dangerous bend with a terrifying drop-off, I saw stones flying out from the back tire and bounding down the side of the precipice. The rear of the car skidded to the outside, I began to pray in earnest, but Lonnie never even noticed—he kept right on talking, looking at me, and smiling.

Lonnie Hardin and Father Marcian were the two non–Indian residents on the reservation with whom I had the most contact. Lonnie and his family gushed southern warmth and hospitality, but he could be quite businesslike when the need arose. At the end of my second year at Whitetail, Lonnie reluctantly told me that the children were not testing well. When that happened, it was understood that the teacher was at fault. Lonnie suggested that I might want to try some other line of work, adding that if I did, he would allow me to leave with a good rating. I appreciated both his candidness and his availabilty anytime I needed him, and I had always known in my heart that I lacked the skills needed to teach elementary school. But when he put the obvious into words, I knew instantly how painful it would be to leave the kids, their parents and grandparents, and the friends I had made on the reservation. Art Blazer was one of those special people.

I first saw Art at the cow camp, the center of the thriving cattle business run by the Chiricahua Apaches, where he was the foreman. His family's long history of association with the people on the Mescalero Apache Reservation dated back to the late 1800s when Art's great-grandfather, a dentist, moved to the edge of the reservation. Unable to make a living from dentistry, he built a mill, became a trader to the Apaches, and earned a reputation as a fair and honest man whose word could be trusted.

Blazer's Mill is mentioned often in the annals of New Mexico history because of a gun battle fought there in April, 1878, during the Lincoln County War, when some of Dr. Blazer's guests got into a roiling, broiling argument. That sort of thing was hardly exceptional in the Old West, except that one of the participants in this battle was Billy the Kid. One man was shot between the eyes and another had a finger blown off, according to Blazer, who recently retold the story to me as I sat in the spacious living room of his ranch house on a beautiful hilltop site outside Capitan, New Mexico. Art's grandfather and father stayed at the mill through the years and followed in their ancestor's footsteps. Because of the respect each earned from the Apaches, Art was trusted to help with the Chiricahuas' thriving cattle business.

I first met Art at a neighbor's house near the teacherage, having previously seen him only at a distance. At that time he was married to the neighbor's daughter and was already a collector of Apache artifacts and other treasures, including an old .44 said to have belonged to Billy the Kid. He let some of us try it behind the school. We threw up small pieces of wood to see if we could hit them. That old gun had such a kick that it nearly flew out of my hand when I gave it a try. In my opinion, nobody could have hit a barn with that weapon, much less put holes in coins thrown in the air, as Billy was supposed to have done.

Today Art Blazer's walls are covered with artwork and priceless curios, some of them handed down in his family for more than a century. Along with his knowledge about the objects from the Chiricahuas' material culture, Art knows quite a lot about the history of the people, and he was a friend to all in the old Whitetail community. He speaks about that long affiliation with the distinctive New Mexico drawl that one would expect from an old-time ranch hand. Art still dresses like a cowpoke and has retained the cowboy's lean, rangy look. His weather-beaten face has a few more wrinkles than it had when we were buddies at Whitetail, but a big smile can easily erase all those traces of his outdoor life.

The Blazers were related through marriage to the Landries (Art married their daughter), the only non-Indian family at Whitetail that had not married into the Apaches. Bill Landrie, Sr., was in charge of providing water for the livestock and keeping the community's sole source of water functioning. Occasionally he asked me to check the well and see if the motor needed more gas. Then up the side of the high storage tank I would climb, peering down with a flashlight to measure the water level. When it was too low, I could see the exit pipe, and I knew what would soon be flowing into the community's homes: ghastly brown water with a peculiar smell, at best. At worst, as I mentioned earlier, the faucets would spit out solid objects such as parts of dead birds that had been floating in the tank.

The Landrie house at Whitetail was larger than those of the Chiricahuas and it had a few more refinements than even the teacherage. Mrs. Landrie was a fine cook, and my wife and I never refused an invitation to eat supper with them. While she served the food (usually chicken, her specialty), Bill would regale us with stories from his childhood, only some of which were true. Art Blazer had warned me that Bill loved to stretch the truth to make a good story even more interesting.

A favorite tale of mine was about the Landries' freeloading relatives, who would come, uninvited, from their home in Georgia about once a year to visit for a week or two. Bill said he got tired of it one year and decided to do something about it. Mrs. Landrie nailed metal pie plates to the old ranch table after a big turkey dinner and then served dessert. When the relatives made their usual unenthusiastic offers to help clean up, Mrs. Landrie told them not to worry. She opened the screen door and whistled for the dogs, who rushed in, jumped up on the table, and licked off all the plates. The guests packed their belongings and left in a hurry.

After I got to know them, the Landries told me why they left the South and never intended to return. Bill, Sr., had a childhood friend who was black. When both were about twelve years old, his friend laughed or whistled at a white girl. The news got out, and some of the older men in the community dragged the young boy away to teach him a lesson. They tied him to a stake and burned him alive. Bill was made to watch, and he never forgot the shrieks and cries of his friend as he died. He said he wanted no part of such a vicious, primitive society. Even though Apaches were far from being nonviolent, Bill felt they were much more civilized.

Jimmy Landrie was the teenage son of the family, and he and I shared a couple of common interests. We both liked card games, and every now and then I called him to see if he wanted to spend an evening playing cards. The young fellow was often bored, so he was usually willing. Occasionally, my wife and I would wander up to the Landrie house and sit around with the family, sharing stories and munching on pretzels or whatever goodies Mrs. Landrie turned out of her oven. She baked often in the winter to warm the kitchen without wasting propane. It was a precious commodity at Whitetail, and I believe many of the Chiricahuas were as frugal, if not more so. Sometimes Jimmy and I would go into the teacherage's basement to turn something on the lathe. When the Shop Smith came our way, we made picture frames galore, until the unseasoned wood that we cut from the Whitetail forest began to warp.

Miles McCoy and his family, transplanted Texans from Lubbock, managed the local ten-cent store in town and were like second parents to me. Miles was a handsome fellow in his forties, blind in one eye. He had been an executive for an oil company before World War II. He quit his well-paying job when he heard there was a shortage of defense workers and went to work as a welder in Los Angeles. An idealist, he became disenchanted when the union steward complained that he was working too hard and too fast, throwing the quota system off. Worse, his skill forced all the other employees to work harder and faster. Miles felt betrayed, but he stayed on and saved his money for a few years. When he had enough in the bank, he quit his job in California, moved his family to Ruidoso, and bought the little store.

At the end of the 1940s Ruidoso was still a wide-open western town that saw its share of violence every day. When the Lincoln County sheriff (whose name I have forgotten) visited Ruidoso, he routinely had lunch at the local pharmacy, a quaint log structure with almost enough room to move around once a person was inside. In addition to the usual drugstore items and a few souvenirs for sale, a little slot machine sat unobtrusively near the door. Whenever I dropped a nickel in the slot, it generously repaid me, causing the pharmacist, a Mr. Cook, great consternation. He and the sheriff discussed the odd occurrence and always wondered if the machine was broken, but Cookie never did anything about it.

The sheriff was a tall, skinny fellow who looked a little like television lawman Matt Dillon, although this was before *Gunsmoke,* of course. He loved to tell stories at the lunch counter—not about the Chiricahuas living atop the mountain, but about the tourists. Once he described a couple of fellows who got drunk and started a fight in front of the local saloon. One man knocked the other to the ground and literally gouged his eyes out before the sheriff could get there. As if that was not bad enough, the sheriff also said that he picked up at least one body a week in back of the racetrack, just outside town. He also complained about the tourists bringing their guns into Ruidoso and shooting up the tavern after belting down a few rounds of hard stuff. Back then, the tourists thought they owned the town and could do as they pleased, which was fairly close to the truth. That was all right with the local physician, Larry Moore, M.D. The tourists' appetite for violence and the consequences of the locals' social lives kept him hopping.

Larry told us that wife swapping was rampant among some of Ruidoso's leading citizens, and he knew of several clubs where wives were traded for a night or so. Socially transmitted diseases were the main medical consequences of the wife swapping, but despite Larry's dire warnings to his patients, the practice continued. It is safe to say that none of the Apaches participated in these activities, not only because they were unwelcome in such situations, but also because of the ancient cultural ramifications of such behavior: the wife might have the tip of her nose cut off.[16]

Just before I arrived at Whitetail, an Apache man came home one night and found his wife in bed with another man. Someone who had seen it soon afterward described the scene to me. The wife's nose was left undisturbed, but her side had been ripped open by a shotgun blast. Bloody handprints along the outside wall of the house ended in a long finger smear at the site where the wounded woman had fallen to the ground. There she lay with her lifeblood pouring out around her. Inside the house, the head of her Mexican lover had rolled under the bed, blown off by the same gun.

More than likely, Dr. Moore was not called to Whitetail for this medical emergency, or any others like it, although he was the physician who treated me for the amebic dysentery I picked up from the Whitetail water. His intervention saved my life, but he, unfortunately, died at the early age of forty, a few years after we left. One day his wife found him dead, sitting in a chair, perhaps fulfilling a worry that he confided to me: reliable statistics showed that country doctors lived an average of only ten years after they left medical school. Medical practice in the rural areas was just too taxing, he explained.

The Mescalero Reservation provided a good example of why healing the sick in remote areas usually involved much more than a physical examination, diagnosis, treatment and prescriptions, and subsequent follow-up visits. Back in the days when doctors made house calls, they often had to travel for hours across wild, unbroken terrain to reach an ailing patient. It required lots of time and a vehicle able to withstand the punishment. If the injury had resulted from a violent confrontation, there was always a chance that the physician himself might be injured, that the argument that caused the initial bloodshed had not been satisfactorily settled and that the doctor's intervention might make him a part of the problem.

There were many deaths and mysterious disappearances on the reservation in those days. Half the children in my grade school had lost one or both parents, and no one could (or would) tell me where the missing people might be. I never forgot about this during my years away from Whitetail, and when I spoke to one of my former students in 1992, I brought up the subject again. He hedged and obviously declined to talk about it, neither denying nor confirming the disappearances. It may be that some of those who vanished joined the bands that still roamed as late as 1954. Perhaps they became part of the "lost" Apaches who are said to have escaped the U.S. Army in 1886 and to have fled to Mexico's Sierra Madre. Or perhaps the death or disappearance was the result of an accident.

I recall an incident that occurred as I was changing reels during one of the Friday night movies at the school. A man rushed in and said that there had been an accident just down the road. Someone had been killed, and the man needed to use the telephone at the school to call in the report. According to him, the car had hit a rock in the road and bounced into the ditch. One of the occupants had tried to jump out but was caught between the door and the car as he jumped. He was crushed to death when the car tipped on its side, closing the door against him. The other four passengers, who had leaped to safety, tried but failed to push the car back upright. It sounded horrible. Along with others, I went to the site to try to help, but I could not see much in the blackness, even with my flashlight. After a great deal of discussion and agreement that there was nothing to be done, we all went home and trusted that the "authorities," to whom the accident had been reported, would take care of the situation sometime during the night.

The next morning I arose early and went back to the scene of the accident. No one else was there, and the body had been removed, apparently by the "authorities." I walked up the road looking for the rock that had thrown the car out of control, but I found no rock and saw no skid marks or other evidence of an accident. I did, however, see signs that a car had backed into the ditch. The next thing I noticed was that the ditch bank was not very steep, and, from where the car was resting, one strong Apache could have pushed it back upright.

With mounting suspicions about foul play, and considering myself to be a good citizen, I called Lonnie Hardin, my supervisor. After carefully listening to my description of the entire situation, he told me to forget it. The worst that could happen was that some of the fellows in the car would spend a couple of weeks in jail, but any further action on my part would stir up bad feelings against me. I quickly dropped it, realizing that I had just learned invaluable lessons in Apache justice and in minding my own business.

I had another experience with Apache justice when I spent a day in tribal court. The brother of one of my students had broken into the school and stolen some food. My duty was to report the theft and then to be a witness at the legal proceedings. I convinced myself that hauling this young fellow before the tribal judge was in his best interest because it would end his potential life of crime and that he would be taught a lesson.

I was the first witness called to testify, and I recited the facts as I knew them: the window had been broken, the pantry was a mess because the foodstuffs had been rifled, and some items were missing. Then it was the judge's turn to question me. He asked how much a loaf of bread cost and how many slices were missing. Because I had no answer for that or for any of his other inquiries in the detail he demanded, he threw the case out of court. I felt as if I were the criminal, convicted and castigated for even bothering to mention the incident. After all, I rationalized, the boy was hungry and just wanted a little food. What was wrong with that? I should just have kept my mouth shut.

I remained in the courtroom for a few minutes while the embarrassed blush on my face subsided and happened to hear the next case. An Apache woman from Whitetail and her thirteen-year-old daughter had been accused of prostitution. The judge asked her why two cowboys were in her home on a certain night. It was very cold that night, the woman explained, and the men had stopped in on their way back to the cow camp. The hour being late, she did not want to be inhospitable or to cause them to get lost or suffer frostbite, so she invited them to stay. Then the judge got to the heart of the matter. He asked why the cowboys had not slept separately from her and her daughter. There were only two beds, she said. Why, then, the judge asked, didn't she and her daughter sleep in one bed and the two cowboys in the other? The laughter from the spectators in the courtroom was so loud that I could hardly hear the verdict and punishment—a slight reprimand and an admonition not to get caught doing it again.

I knew the woman quite well and liked her. She was about forty years old, round as a tub, and pleasant. I remember dancing with her one night and being surprised that the other women rushed to my wife to warn her that I might fall madly in love and run off with this woman.

It was virtually impossible to enforce the law on the reservation. For example, there was a house just around the sharp bend in the road where gambling was said to occur. The sheriff and I tried to design a strategy to catch the culprits in the act, but we never did. I was involved because my duties included keeping a lid on this and other illegal behaviors, but having been the target of Apache humor in the past, I wanted to see the gambling for myself before I tried to do anything about it. I discussed with my bus driver how I might sneak up to the window and shoot a picture of the operation. Then I discovered that pictures taken through glass would not stand up in tribal court. I was frustrated. Perhaps most important was the problem of getting to the house unobserved by the gamblers inside. The place sat in the middle of a large open space. If the occupants saw me approaching, all the incriminating evidence would have disappeared by the time I reached the door. If I managed to make it undetected and shot a picture, how could I escape the angry Apaches and do anything with the photo? I gave up, and the gambling continued.

Justice has many guises, and I learned a bit about United States government justice during my time at Whitetail. A few Apaches told me that just after the first A-bomb test in July, 1945, at White Sands Missile Range, a huge military installment less than fifty miles from the Mescalero Apache Reservation,[17] their sheep on the western slopes of the hillsides began dying. The cows survived—probably, the people believed, because they ate only the top of the grass, whereas the sheep ate it much closer to the ground. When the people complained to the government about losing their herds, they were told that the deaths could not possibly be from radioactivity, but no one would explain why only the sheep grazing on the western slopes (the ones facing White Sands) were affected. No attempt was made to reimburse the Apaches for their losses.

Remuneration was always a topic of interest to the Apaches. One day a lawyer from the Bureau of Indian Affairs came to Whitetail to arrange hearings on the Apaches' land claims. According to the people, their homeland covered an area from Mexico north into Colorado, and included most of New Mexico and Arizona. Since the Chiricahuas had been nomads and did not measure property or think in terms of land ownership, the entire subject of remuneration by the government for the land taken from them was enormously complicated. The initial meetings went on for a few days, attended mostly by Chiricahua men, including the leaders Eugene Chihuahua, Asa Daklugie, Robert Geronimo, Charley Smith, Jr., and Charlie Istee. A few women attended from time to time, and I recall one in particular—Dahteste.

The lawyer met with older members of the Whitetail community who could remember the days before captivity. The meetings were held in one room at the school and were in English. Dahteste refused to speak English, so someone translated for her. The government man asked her where she was born and when. She said, as I recall, that she had been born near what is now Phoenix, Arizona, but she did not know the exact date. She thought it was about one hundred years ago. The lawyer asked her if she had ever gone with a raiding party into Phoenix. She said something in Apache and every Chiricahua in the room laughed. The translator said, "I'm just born and already I'm making raids?" To the Indians it was very funny because, in the Apache way, one takes things in chronological order, rather than skipping around. If the lawyer had known that, he might have asked first about her early childhood and youth, or, better yet, would have waited patiently for her to unfold her life story in her own words. But he was in a hurry to get to the point, as are most non-Indians. While he wanted to get back to Washington, though, the Apaches had plenty of time. On the other hand, the government did take its time in reimbursing the Chiricahuas for the loss of their land.

Who can say whether these and other injustices caused some of the people such pain that they looked for something, anything, to alleviate the anguish? I remember that drinking was a constant problem while I was at Whitetail. During those days it was still illegal to sell liquor to Indians, but the stuff was readily available. A store just off the reservation sold it, and every weekend some Apaches could be found dead drunk beside the road.

As the tribal police had no jurisdiction off the reservation, and the county sheriff had no interest in getting involved, the place remained open. When per capita payments or money from the sale of crops or stock came in, a few folks would disappear for a while. They would come back stripped of their wealth and reduced to poverty until the next payments arrived. I hoped and prayed that the students sitting so innocently in my classroom would not grow up to become like the alcoholics they saw in their community. My hopes were in vain. Many of my students followed that path, and many were dead from alcoholism when I at long last returned to the reservation in 1992.

Chapter 6
Talks with the Kids and the Cook

One of the unexpected delights of recording these recollections was that a few of the students, now fully grown, also wanted to get into the act. Henrietta and I had always planned to talk with my former students to confirm certain memories, but we were really happy to learn that some were willing to tell us about their own memories, hopes, traditions, and worries.

My conversations with Vernon Simmons and Berle and Lynette Kanseah, and with the Whitetail school's former cook, Dorcie Kazhe, were strictly informal and followed no prescribed pattern, and our efforts to fit what they so willingly told me into some sort of structural format were not entirely successful. Not incidentally, I should point out that the information gleaned from several discussions with Vernon, Dorcie, Berle, and Lynette derives from their subjective remembrances of people they knew and events that happened nearly fifty years ago. If conflicting recollections exist, chalk them up to differing perspectives. Their words illuminate a small segment of the little-known true history of the Chiricahua Apaches. By providing a glimpse inside their culture, Vernon, Dorcie, Berle, and Lynette have made an invaluable contribution to American history.

Vernon Simmons

Vernon Simmons is the grandson of Eugene Chihuahua's Comanche wife, Hernannie,[1] but he is also related to many Chiricahuas. Eugene and Hernannie eventually divorced, and she left Whitetail and returned to her home in Oklahoma. Vernon, however, stayed at Whitetail and continued to live with his step-grandfather. His most treasured recollections are of the Chiricahua Apache people at Whitetail and their traditions.

Remembering Charlie Istee, the son of Chief Victorio, Vernon said,

> I was taking Melvin [Kanseah] home once on horseback. It was about four o'clock in the afternoon and I rode along a short cut behind the graveyard—the path that comes out right in the field where Charlie and them lived. The old man Charlie was standing by the gate. He knew where I lived and called, "Are you going home? Why don't you come on in and eat with us? We're going to eat pretty soon." I was getting hungry and was about ready. They had those big old hard tin cups you put hot coffee in. They poured me one. The only time I drank coffee was with Eugene and my grandma. Anyway, they gave me a tin plate like a pie plate. They were eating meat. I don't know if it was deer meat or beef, probably beef. [Charlie's wife] gave me a big piece and I sat there looking at it. Didn't have a fork, or a knife, or anything to eat with. All of a sudden Charlie pulled his pocket knife out from a little satchel he had on the side of his pants. He used his hand to hold the meat and cut it. He looked at me and said, "Use your hands! We don't have no fork and spoon, and that's not the way to eat anyway." He cut the meat with his knife, put it in his mouth, and sat there eating it. In Apache, he told his wife to bring me a knife and fork, so she did, but he still said, "Use your hands to eat with. . . . You eat better with your hands . . . it tastes better." I could only drink about half of the coffee. It was real hot and pretty strong. Later I got on my horse and rode back past the school and the church, behind Naiche's house, and came on home.

Another of Vernon's memories concerns liver and kidneys:

> We had an outhouse, a barn, and a chicken house. People would go to town once a month and buy slabs of bacon. The slabs came in gunnysacks and they'd hang the bacon in the barn where it was cool. We raised potatoes, radishes, cabbage, and corn. A lot was canned. I grew up eating liver. Deer liver. My grandmother used to cook it and put a little brown gravy on it. Onions too. But she didn't serve it every day. Maybe the others were taught not to eat deer liver because I hardly ever saw anyone else eating it.
>
> I remember when I first ate a piece of kidney. They [the Apache cowboys] were butchering and had a big fire going. During branding they probably killed a couple of cows. After butchering, they pulled those kidneys out (I think it was four or six) and kind of washed them with water a little bit and threw them on the coals. Kenoi was cooking and just kept watching and turning them over with a stick. Clarence Enjady said, "They're done! I know. I can smell it." He took out a pocket knife and plucked them off the fire. "Gimme some salt," he said. Everybody ate with salt then. I still do today. He cut the kidney and ate it. "That's done," he called in Indian. "Go help yourself." I liked it. Still today, if I get a chance, that's the way I like to cook fresh

kidneys. My son likes them that way too, but not my daughter. She won't eat them. Anything you cook outside tastes better to me.

Vernon Simmons was close to Dahteste and helped her with her chores, especially as she grew older. He remembered her as I did, riding along the dirt road on the back of her burro, clip clopping slowly to wherever she was going, never in a hurry. Vernon recalled one special spring day when he was sitting with Dahteste on her porch:

She saw an eagle flying across [the treetops] above the Whitetail school. She looked at him and said, "I bet he looked good on the mountain. You know, when I was a little girl traveling somewhere that way—somewhere west—there's a mountain we used to use. Almost looked like twin peaks. Cochise used to use that as a landmark where we would have to turn right or left. You can't miss it," she said. "It's maybe a hundred miles from here, maybe two hundred, going toward the west."

Well, it really is about 150 miles west. Some time back, I was coming around a curve near Deming, New Mexico, just driving. I happened to look and it just clicked. There it was. I hit my brakes, stopped, and got out of the car. My wife thought something happened to the car. I walked back a little and looked where I could really see it good. It clicked again. Right away. That old lady . . . what she said . . . the peaks looked exactly alike. Right in front of me was the landmark to turn right or left. When they saw that, the Chiricahuas knew how close they were to where they had to go. I told my wife, "That old lady at Whitetail was telling me about this. We saw an eagle flying and she was talking about mountains. That's when it came up." And right to this day you can go to that spot. Every time I drive to see my sister in Arizona, I make a five-minute stop to show my kids what the old lady told me. You can't miss it.[2]

A lot of the old ones were converted [to Christianity] in Fort Sill. Eugene told me that, and I think he was converted too. I remember after a talk we had about religion and he said, "I don't care what you call me but don't ever call me 'father.' Tell your kids not to call you father because you only have one father" and he was talking about God Almighty. I tell my kids that right now.

Eugene used to get up about four or five o'clock in the morning, maybe earlier than that. I'd ask Grandma where he was going. She said he was going to pray. But I know he didn't go to church that early in the day. Once I asked him about it. He said he prayed because we needed rain. I don't forget these little things. On the porch he told me, "There's something you do as a duty when you're in the city or somewhere else. If you want help, call to your father in heaven. Get out of the city, go find some trees, mountains, birds. Get up early in the morning. Go out there and pray like you're really praying for something. The churches are coming into Mescalero. It's a different way they teach, but it's all the same God, all the same father. You could go to all of them but it's meant for us to go into the woods."

Eugene told me a lot about the Apache religion. When he went out to pray, God talked to him. He came back one time and said, "God was kinda mad at me today." Never did find out what he really meant. In speaking of God, Eugene told me, "You can't see Him, but He's there in spirit. He's all around. I can feel it." I asked Eugene, "When you go out to the woods and pray to God the Father, do you pray in English?" He said he didn't because God understands everybody.

One time we were having a feast [the traditional puberty ceremony] and it was raining. After that, a rainbow came out and it cleared up. You could see the sun real good, but then the clouds came in again and it started to rain while the sun was out. Old Lady Coonie [Dahteste] said in Apache, "The devil's whippin' his wife." And I looked all around. Clarence Enjady was standing nearby and laughed. He put his arm around me and told me that when the sun was out and it was raining, the old Apaches believed the devil was whipping his wife. As I look back and think about that Old Lady Coonie, she was never converted [to modern ways]. She stayed the old way, did things in the old way. She chopped wood, she butchered, she cut her own meat—all of what her mother and grandmother taught her. Handed down. When I was a little boy, she still did things the old way. I never saw a man doing anything for her. She did it all herself.

The puberty ceremony Vernon mentioned was a gift to all the Apache people from White Painted Woman, a powerful deity. "There shall be songs for the girls," she decreed. "During this feast the *Gah'e* shall dance in front. After that there shall be round dancing and face to face dancing."[3] All Apaches have a personal place in their hearts for the *Gah'e*, the Mountain Spirit dancers. These representations of deities have accompanied the people through untold hardships and humiliation and have been close at hand to enjoy and share in the people's successes. The dancers are intensely spiritual; they connect the Apache people with their origins and with a world few outsiders are privileged to understand. They usually appear at special occasions, walking single file out of the darkness toward a blazing bonfire. Bare-chested, wearing moccasins and fringed yellow buckskin skirts with jingles, they shuffle toward the fire. On their heads, which are covered with black cloths, they wear the magnificent headdresses that resemble wooden crowns, with tall, painted spikes that penetrate the night. In their hands they hold short staffs painted with the symbols of a people long persecuted yet vital, resilient, and rich in heritage. Pointing at the fire, they slowly dance toward it, followed by a clown who hops and skips, acting as if he is not part of the group.

The *Gah'e* circle the blaze to their left at first and then approach the fire from the four directions, still in a line, still moving their feet in a symbolic step. They make a sound that is not a cry, not a moan, not an imitation of a bird's call; it is a call to or from the spirit world rather than an earthly harmonic. They dance most of the night, pounding the earth with ancient choreography passed through the invisible curtain to them from the spirit world.

Each dancer has his chest and arms painted in symbolic designs that have great relevance to Apache tradition. Vernon recalled standing on his porch and overhearing Eugene Chihuahua and Richard Johlsanny working out a design for the dancers' chests while sitting on the ground: "The old man [Johlsanny] had a stick and he was drawing [in the dirt] with it. 'This is what you got to use, Eugene,' he said. It was a star. Then he reversed it. Black and white, white and black. 'That's good,' the old man said. 'That helps a lot.' Now they use it today. It's still here. It's what he just drew on the ground and I was standing right there."

Vernon had a few memories about other incidents related to the spiritual aspects of Chiricahua traditional ways. In particular, he recalled watching the construction of a box in which to bury medicine man Eugene Chihuahua's ceremonial paraphernalia, apparently after Eugene had stopped using it. The clothing and ritual objects he used as a healer could not be passed on and were buried with a ceremony in a secret place somewhere at Whitetail. During this discussion Vernon hesitated frequently, perhaps worried that he was giving away too much information. When his doubts began to overtake him, he hurriedly emphasized that he would never tell the location of the box. Then he continued:

> Bruce Klinekole, Sr., brought lumber for Eugene and that's the way he started building the box. They unloaded it at the barn. "I brought you nails and an extra hammer and stuff like that," Klinekole said. I was standing right there and didn't pay much attention to it. And then he left. Then [medicine man] Charley Smith came, and Asa [Daklugie] and Christian [Naiche, son of Cochise] and Richard Johlsanny. He was sort of a little man to me. They put the box together that afternoon, fixed it, and buried it.
>
> They kept some things away from me because I was little, but I remember the season we went piñon picking. Camped out. The old ladies would sit there and talk

about certain medicine and say there was no use in getting real sick because it was a long way to the hospital. "Here," they'd say, "This stuff will cure you better. Try some of this. Get under a blanket with this . . . smell the smoke."

One time I got bit by a horsefly at the cow camp. They'd bite and suck blood out of you. Your arm hurts and swells. Everyone wore long sleeves, but I had a T-shirt on and two of them horseflies bit me. I was going to slap my arm, but one of the medicine women grabbed me by the shoulders and said in Apache, "Do not touch it." Then she took me to where the cattle were drinking water, ten, maybe fifteen yards away. There was a mud hole there, and she scooped out some mud. Then she spit on it. She put it on my arm, just like that. She said, "Don't worry. It will go away pretty soon." She sat holding me for ten minutes, just watching it. All of a sudden she let go of me and said, "Get on your horse now. Ride around. Go back home. Everybody's going, anyway." By the time I got to my house all that mud came off and the bite was gone. No swelling, either.

It was simple the way they did it. Look at the [first-aid] spray used today. Costs ten dollars maybe. Maybe less. But the mud was free. You just go there and get it. We had a remedy for warts, too. Stinkbugs. If I got a wart, I just put a stinkbug on it. Corns on your toes? Try stinkbugs. They make you smell pretty bad—out of this world—but they'll cure you if you have warts or corns. But don't kill the stinkbug. Just rub him on there and when you're through, put him back down on the ground. He did his work. You'll smell awful, but it works. I use it on my kids and they don't have warts. Or corns.

My wife knows a little about Indian medicine. When she has a bad cold and can't get rid of it, she lights something, burns it, puts a blanket over her head, and inhales it for a while. Younger kids nowadays don't like the old ways because they're brought up the other way. But if all this is not recorded, fifty years from now no one will know the real story.

I used to go out to the old graveyard in Whitetail. I remember it took almost a week to dig a grave out there because it's so rocky. [When somebody died] Eugene got on a horse every morning after breakfast and said, "We gotta get that grave finished today." He'd be gone all day. And then one day they said to me, "You stay home today. We know you think you should go, but you don't understand this yet. Someday I'll tell you about it. Someday you'll learn these things." I remember Eugene saying the same, "You'll learn all these things." If there were kids there [at the cemetery during a burial], they were lucky.

Now I know where the graves are, even if they are unmarked. Eugene is buried in Mescalero, but I wish they would have buried him at Whitetail. A lot of those people needed to be buried at Whitetail. Berle's [Kanseah] mother can tell you about a lot of *those places where people are buried at Whitetail. She's about the last one left. I don't like to be pushy, but I said to James, Berle's boy, "Now's your chance. Your grandma's getting pretty old. I hate to tell you this but go ask her a lot of these questions. Learn these things they're telling you. They're going to be lost. Ask her. You know, she might tell you more than she told your daddy because your grandpa [in western society's kinship terminology, Vernon meant James's great-grandfather, Jasper Kanseah, Sr., nephew of Geronimo], he's not here, you know." If my Grandmother was living, I'd get her into a room with a little recorder and ask, 'Who was your momma? Your grandpa? Where did they come from?' All that's leaving us. There's so many good stories that I learned. Sometimes when my wife and I are in bed and she's reading, she reads me part of a book about the Chiricahuas when they were running somewhere. "Did you hear it like that?" she asks. Sometimes I say, "Pretty close, but no." Other times I say, "Who's the son of a bitch who wrote that?" I may have been told something like that, but not the way it's told in the book. It's not the way it was told to me when they were living; I mean the time I was a little boy.*

When Vernon was a child, the government housing provided for the Chiricahuas at Whitetail was nothing but thin boards slapped together with whatever filler was handiest. None were insulated against the harsh winters at more than eight thousand feet above sea level. The Chihuahua house that Vernon shared with his Comanche grandmother and Eugene Chihuahua had only four rooms,

but they looked huge to me. The living room was big and they [the adults] had a bedroom. You went in the back and they had a kitchen and another bedroom. There were two closets, one on the bed side and one on the other side. [The house] had an attic. There was a little hole up there and they took stuff up. I remember when the electricity was coming in. Guys had to crawl around up in the attic. My grandmother had to move things around; the guys made holes in the wall. They put poles up first with the high lines and then brought it to the house. A long time after they put the poles in—maybe six months to a year, maybe even a year and a half, it was late summer—they went house to house putting light fixtures in. Took about three days.

We used to have coal, hauled up on a truck. We'd get all black using it. I remember pumping by hand when we had the old generator. It had numbers on it and went up to five gallons. All the Apache boys used to pump it. I'll never forget the color. Red. It was red gasoline. Red gasoline. Can you imagine that?

The houses were in real bad shape, and the men had to go to town to buy lumber to repair them. There was no bathroom inside. Our outhouse had two holes, I know. I remember that. And then there was a barn and chicken house. We had chickens . . . didn't have to worry about eggs. Some people in Whitetail were so poor they didn't have any. . . .

Mentioning chickens brought to mind other animals owned and used by the Chiricahuas at Whitetail, which in turn, led along strings of memories to subjects, some long forgotten but dear to his heart. And to other subjects as well, in particular to the taboos about owls carried through the generations by the Chiricahua Apaches.

In traditional beliefs the owl is one of the strongest forms a ghost can take to frighten the living, and owls are thought to be the spirits of evil persons. A well-known tale about an owl concerns a man whose wife had died. The widower continued to live at the same location, though he avoided using the spot where she had died. One night he heard knocking at the door. Then something called him by name. He went to the door but could see no one. The same thing happened for three nights running. He was very frightened and kept his gun ready.

On the fourth night there was a full moon. While in bed the man thought he heard a rapping on the window. He looked and was pretty sure he saw his wife's face. He tried to talk to her. He said, "Come in at the door if you have anything to say to me, let us see each other face to face." But no one came in.

After a while he heard the rapping again. This time he shot, and he heard groans. He was afraid to go outside until morning. When he did go out, he found a dead owl lying by the window. The next day he told the story. He knew he would not live long after that, and he was right. He could have gone to an owl shaman, but he did not care much about going on living after that.[4] "I was taught you leave them alone," Vernon stated about owls, adding,

> That's what Eugene and the old ladies said, and I believed them. If you hear coyotes . . . or bears . . . and they're hungry, you don't bother them. If you see them before they see you, they won't bother you, but always carry a gun. That's what I was taught.
>
> Once at the crack of dawn (we could still see the stars) we got up and Eugene built a fire in the living room heater. Then my Grandma got up and they were talking in the bedroom. I slept in there with them. Grandma got me an extra blanket and I heard Eugene say, "Did you hear those coyotes hollerin' all night? Somethin' gonna

happen real bad." The next day he said, "I'm gonna find out what happened." He got on his horse and rode off. Came back about ten o'clock and said somebody had died. I didn't know who it was, though.

We also believe that someone's going to die if there's a bird in the house. I remember an Apache went to a friend's place and heard some chirping. He told the friend, "Get out of here," and she got up and left right away.

As a member of Eugene Chihuahua's family, Vernon heard a lot about the historic events that had so devastated the Chiricahua Apaches:

I was born in this world fighting and running. What land my forefathers had, we tried to keep. The soldiers kept trying to get more and more. And it was ours, all ours. If they'd come and asked us for it, asked for it like it should have been asked for, we probably would have given them some. They just had to come and kill and take it away. You've also got to remember that we were not all that good either, but before all this happened, from what I was told by my grandpa, we were already here. We were doing good. We didn't have disease. We didn't get sick. . . .

Hugh Coonie was drinking one time and he was telling me about his daddy [the scout Kuni, last husband of Dahteste]. Kuni told him what they went through down in Mexico. He said they met Mexicans, some good, some no good. The good ones they left alone. When they crossed the border into the United States, they had to fight the cavalry and they didn't like any of them. They were all the same. Coonie said that his father was a scout out in front of Cochise. Kuni was two or three days ahead of Cochise's band and anything he saw he would come back and report. One time he and another scout were way out and came to an arroyo. The cavalry was on both sides and Kuni was stuck in the middle. He had left his horse up on the mountain and couldn't get to it. The army men got to drinking and after a while Kuni crawled up under a wagon and saw a gunnysack on the back of a mule. He took it off real gently so the mule never did move. Kuni stole some food, ammunition, and whiskey and put everything in the sack. He crawled between the army's coaches and got away, just walked right back up that hill to his horse. He told Cochise he could have leaned over and cut the boots off those cavalry men.

Whenever Vernon wants to feel better about everything, he drives to Whitetail:

When I go up there, I'm so happy. I'm just so comfortable, I'm home. And I can picture that yellow school bus parked over there and the green pickup at the school, and the garage door open, and that cattle guard there with the sign that said WHITETAIL DAY SCHOOL. It's gone now and I don't know where it is. My kids don't believe me when I tell them about the sign. The sign had an Indian wearing a long-feathered headdress carved into the wood, but we Apaches never wore those. The government didn't know that. I tell my kids that on this side of the road was a big yellow barn. They kept hay or oats in it and right next to it was a tin shack, I think, where they kept the tractor and the combine. Right next to that was Bill Landrie's house, and then on the righthand side is where the Kanes used to live. When you passed it, next was Hugh Coonie's house, and then the next one was Hugh Chee, and the next one was the church. There was a big tree right there. As soon as you get over the hill, that's where Barney Naiche and his wife, Rosalie, lived. You went past it a little bit and on the lefthand side was Maude and Robert Geronimo's house. Asa Daklugie was up above that. Old Lady Coonie's house had an old rusty car parked in the field, just down from Charlie Istee's place.

And those big rocks out in the field—we used to play there. Cowboys and Indians. . . .

Dorcie Kazhe

Dorcie Kazhe, my second cook, was a Pima-Papago Indian woman who met her future husband, a Chiricahua Apache named Isaac Kazhe, at the Phoenix, Arizona, Indian School. Dorcie remembered the school well:

> The school was like a military academy. It was way back in the twenties when I was seven or eight years old. In those days they had strict military training in boarding school. We were under the merit system. You started out with a hundred [points] and if you were late to class, you got five demerits. We had to earn them back by working our chores or cleaning our room. We had the honor system, had to earn our trust. We wouldn't want to be caught with a dirty room or dirty clothes, so we had to clean our rooms every night before we went to bed and put everything away.
>
> Everyone had to speak English. Some kids came from homes where English wasn't spoken, and they would be punished. They didn't dare talk because they were so scared. A lot of the kids wet their beds, and they were punished too. They were made to stand on the porch holding a placard that said "I wet my bed." Stealing was also punished. I remember that a girl and I once went swimming—we could only go at certain times—and we went into the locker room. The lockers were all identical, and if you had one in the middle you really had to hunt for your locker. Some had numbers on them and some didn't. My friend accidentally opened some else's locker and an envelope fell out. That girl's pictures were all over the floor and my friend got caught putting them back in the envelope. She had to stand in the yard near the fence with a placard that said "I am a thief."
>
> In marching around we all had to keep in step or else we'd get punished for that

also. I attained the high rank of major when I was in school, but was demoted to buck private because of something that happened with a bunch of boys. They formed a chain with their arms and were swinging all around us girls. Someone turned the lights off and the boys knocked us down. I was still trying to get up when the lights came on again; the officials believed I had been lying down with the boys.

Dorcie clearly remembered meeting Ike, her future husband:

Ike was my cousin's boyfriend and they were going to get married, but the girl got pregnant by someone else at a picnic. The relationship fell apart, and then Ike and I got together. We got close and decided to get married. I didn't even know he drank until the night of our wedding. Then I thought, "Well, just go through with it." So we did. I thought after a while he would quit [drinking].

In my tribe we weren't even allowed to hold hands. Papagos chose mates for their children, even when they were small. As a young girl, my mother was already given to a man [but she was permitted to attend school].

Officials used to come along and take the kids far away from their homes. They took my mother and my uncle to school in Carlisle, Pennsylvania. The highest grade in Carlisle was ten, and then they considered themselves graduates. After that my mother got a job at the Pima agency. She taught. And my Dad worked there as a farm boss. I don't know what his title was, but he took care of the farm. They might have gone farther than the tenth grade.

Well, my mother and father met at the agency, and she didn't follow the rule [of marrying the man she was promised to] and she married my father. Her parents never liked my dad. They blamed him for everything. He just wasn't accepted. My grandparents used to tell us kids that we were no good, like our father. I heard stories about my father being an alcoholic and drinking with his cousin. But later on he became a convert [to Christianity]. I'm thankful I never saw my father drunk. I never saw him the way he was pictured. I just saw him as an upright man, always instructing us about the Christian way.

One episode had changed her father's way of life forever:

My father's name was John, and I had a little brother also named John. This little boy seemed to know the time my Dad would come home from work every evening and he'd run to the gate and wait. When my little brother died from falling off his high chair, my father was so overcome with grief that he started crying each time he came home from work. My father's cousin, also named John and a convert, told him, "All you have to do is give your heart to the Lord and when the day comes, you'll be going to your heavenly home and little John will come running to the gate. He'll open the gate for you, but that will not happen if you continue to drink and lead the kind of life you're leading now." That did it.

When Dorcie was eleven years old, her mother died and her father remarried. According to Dorcie, her stepmother was jealous of the children, so two of her sisters were sent to live with relatives and another worked in Phoenix. She recalled:

> A brother and I stayed with them [her father and stepmother]. One evening they went to help another man in his field, and when they came back my father said he wasn't feeling well. He didn't even feel like eating. During the night, after we had fallen asleep, I heard him groaning. He called my brother and me over to his bed and said, "Take the Ford (my brother could drive) and go to Uncle Mark's house. Tell him I'm very sick and to come over." My uncle came back with my brother and decided my father had to go to the hospital, way across the river. My father told my brother and me to stay home and go back to sleep. He told us to be sure to feed the pony, get something to eat, and stay at the house or stay with our sisters or aunts. My father told me I had to stay wherever I was accepted. They had to hurry to take my father away because the Gila River was rising and they had to drive across it. My father never came home from the hospital, and I went to stay with one of my older sisters. From there I went to the Phoenix Indian school.

After leaving school and marrying, Dorcie joined Ike's family at Mescalero. Having been born, raised, and educated in the southern Arizona desert, she experienced something akin to culture shock when Ike brought her to the reservation:

> I'm afraid of snow. It didn't snow back in Arizona, but when I first came here [Mescalero], I looked at the hills and they were covered with snow. And my mother-in-law acted as if I had stolen her prize cat.[5] She didn't even shake hands with me. Ike had wanted me to go to Mescalero earlier, at the end of June, but I didn't want to because I didn't know how the people there were going to treat me. I didn't know them, and I was pregnant then with Carl. I thought I might die at Mescalero and no one would take care of me. So he left me in Tucson and went on ahead. I stayed in Arizona until my son was born, and four months later Ike still hadn't come after us. I should have left him them, but I'm glad I stayed or I never would have had Lynette and Peter. Anyway, on my first Christmas Eve at Mescalero, I was so lonely I just cried and cried. Then I heard caroling somewhere and Ike left. "Just take care of the little boy," he said, "and I'll be back." Oh, I felt so bad. The next day they all stormed in and said they had gone to midnight Mass.

The traditional Apache way calls for the husband to move into the wife's family circle—matrilocality. The domestic family in these circumstances is comprised of the parents, the unmarried sons, the daughters, and the husbands and children of the married daughters. Granddaughters and unmarried grandsons also remain as members of this subgroup, while married grandsons live with their wives' families. Dorcie and Isaac reversed the process. Maybe that's why Dorcie always felt like an outsider, even after she had lived at Whitetail for many years. Or there might have been a historical reason for her feeling, dating back to the days when the Apaches were still a free people. Then, the Pima-Papago tribes in Arizona were bitter enemies of the Apaches and even helped the cavalry track them down and fight them. Some, maybe most, of the Chiricahuas living on the reservation when the new bride arrived may have known of her tribe's actions against them, for Dorcie said she was frequently snubbed, even at the Ladies Aid Society meetings in the small Dutch Reformed church. Dorcie spoke no Apache, which automatically put her at a disadvantage, but she could tell that a few unkind Apache women at the church were making fun of her. Nonetheless, she was a solid enough Christian to remain faithful and continue to participate in the women's group and to attend church services with her family.

Dorcie's relationship with her mother-in-law was never pleasant, even though she and Ike and their son didn't live with Ike's parents. At first the young Kazhe family lived in a dormitory near the center of Mescalero. It was heated in the cold winter months by a big furnace right in the middle of the room, but coal had to be brought in to feed the furnace.

> *I'd get up early, take the coal bucket, get the coal, drag it back, and make the fire. One by one the other people in the dormitory would get up. As I was carrying the coal back one morning I met Sutherland Comanche and asked about his baby, who was very sick. All that time my mother-in-law was watching me, and later she told Ike that I was meeting men down in the coal bin. When Ike came in from his work at the cow camp, he said, "I'm not coming back." And I said, "What are we supposed to do here? You know, Ike, I'm getting tired of it. I can't do what I want to. It seems like I've got to do everything according to what your mother wants." And he said, "What's wrong with that? That's the way it's supposed to be." And I said, "It's not my way."*
>
> *I didn't even have milk for the baby, but the orchard near the dormitory was full of apples. That's what I fed my baby—apple sauce—when I didn't have any milk because the doctor made me take him off the breast.*

> My mother-in-law asked, "Are you ashamed of your breasts? Why did you take him off and put him on the bottle like the white ladies? They don't want to feed their babies, but we Indians, we have to feed our baby." Oh, how she criticized me. I told Ike, "I can't please your mother. I do everything for them. I wash and iron and cook. Everything by hand. No modern conveniences. I can always go back to Arizona." He said he would look into it, and later he came back and said, "I hope you're packed because you're going out to Whitetail. It's way out there. There's nothing out there, but you don't like it here." I got worried. "It's not that I don't like it here," I said. "I just don't like the way I'm treated." So that's how I ended up out at Whitetail. As poor as we were, he took me to one of those cabins that they built for the Chiricahua—it was his mother's cabin—and to me it was heaven. I was so relieved and I settled down there.

But Dorcie Kazhe's troubles with her mother-in-law were far from over, despite the distance between their homes:

> One day she [mother-in-law Emma Toklanni Kazhe] came and brought her two daughters and said they were going to go to school at Whitetail. She dumped them on me. No groceries, nothing. I said to those girls, "I don't know why she left you with me. I never have enough, and I'm supposed to take care of you now?" The girls liked to stay in bed and get up right before the school bus came. I tried to have something warm for them to eat, but they never ate because they'd be so late. Half the time they didn't go to school. Worse, they told their mother that I didn't feed them, and she really got after me.

Despite all the hardships of the new location and the Apaches' snubs, Dorcie remained at Whitetail and raised her children there. I got to know her when she became the cook at the Whitetail school. Dorcie's duties at the school were varied, and she had to be quite flexible. About once a year, for example, she deloused all the kids. On those days she wrapped her hair in a bandanna and wore tight-fitting clothes. One by one, she sat each child on a stool near a window in the school's basement where the sunlight streamed in, as it did almost every afternoon. Dorcie draped a large sheet around the intimidated youngster, making certain the wrap covered the child's clothes. After she tucked the edges closely around the child's neck, she attacked his or her head with a canister of DDT powder. The powder filled the sunlight and formed choking clouds around Dorcie and whoever was on the stool. I remember standing some distance away one time, watching the whole process. She called, "Get back. These cooties can jump a good ten feet!" Then she pointed to them leaping off the kid's head before they disappeared out of sunbeam range. The children didn't seem to mind the process, but it always made everyone itch for several days afterward. These days society is wiser in the consequences of pesticide use, but in the 1940s getting rid of lice with DDT was a proven method.

Chiricahua children by and large had very few problems with vermin. They were usually quite clean and well dressed. There was a shower in both the boys' and the girls' bathrooms at the school, and the kids took one shower a week, two children together to save time and water. Naturally, they got into all sorts of mischief. Dorcie supervised the general activity, but with boys in one shower and girls in the other, her capacity to maintain discipline was limited. If I could, I monitored the boys, especially when their frolicking and whooping made it difficult for me to be heard in the classroom. One day, the ruckus in both showers got so bad that Dorcie and I switched bathrooms. She scrubbed the boys and I scrubbed the girls. Just once was all it took; we never had that trouble again. Nowadays, of course, our solution to the yelling in the showers would be viewed differently than it was back then.

Dorcie's two children, Peter and Lynette, were preschoolers; Peter was older than his sister by a couple of years. They were well mannered, but they were also real characters. Dorcie usually read a Bible story to them once a day. I clearly recall her telling me of one amusing incident. She was going to bathe the kids in the metal wash tub in her kitchen, but first she read them the story of Adam and Eve. Then she asked Lynette to get ready for her bath and left the room. When she returned, both kids had stripped. She looked surprised, so the kids, buck naked, ran out, yelling, "Run, run. Hide in the bushes. Jesus is coming!" One other story stands out in my memory. Again, Dorcie was getting ready to bathe the kids, but they fooled around so much that she was exasperated. "Get in the tub now!" she demanded. "Do you want to be dirty little Indians?" They quieted down and looked at her seriously. "No," one of them said. "We don't want to be dirty like Indians." It had never quite dawned on them that they were Indians, although not dirty ones.

After many years and many experiences, good and bad, Dorcie still resides in Mescalero and is now an elder of eighty-plus years. Ike is dead and her children are grown and married, yet still she stays. A stroke paralyzed the left side of her face, and believes that one of the witches at Mescalero has "witched" her. Before the stroke she was warned about the witch, and she even knew the woman's name, but being a Christian woman, she thought she would not worry about it.

Berle and Lynette Kanseah

Berle is the grandson of Jasper Kanseah, Sr., the youngest of the warriors who surrendered with Geronimo's band, and the son of Jasper Kanseah, Jr. Lynette is the great-granddaughter of Rogers and Siki Toklanni, and the daughter of Dorcie and Isaac Kazhe. Both Berle and Lynette attended the Whitetail Day School, but Lynette was too young to be in the classroom during my tenure. Today, Lynette is an educator on the reservation and Berle is a member of the Mescalero Apache Tribal Council. He is also a spokesman for the Chiricahua Apaches, and he has appeared in film documentaries and gives public lectures about them.

Berle said he remembered the days when the old ways were still observed at Whitetail. "My father observed the mother-in-law relationship with his in-laws,"[6] said Berle, "but with that generation it began changing." That certainly was a break for the husbands. In the old days, a mother-in-law ruled the roost. "Oh, yes," agreed Berle, "Once an Apache man was an in-law to a family, he more or less took care of them. And a man didn't address his in-laws directly. He spoke in the second person. It was a roundabout way. But as we moved away from Whitetail, all those practices started changing. Today we joke about it. We have a lot of fun doing that."

The transition period Berle mentioned was facilitated by a Protestant minister affiliated with the Reformed church at the time, the Rev. Reuben TenHaken. Said Berle:

> He talked about the old people and more or less retold one of the legends, saying the old ways were our people's ways—a wonderful way—a belief in the "Giver of Life," a higher power, more or less parallel to Christianity. He indicated that this was good and cautioned us not to lose it, to hold on to it. After that, in my teenage years I recall he recounted some of the same things, and he also encouraged us to maintain our identity as Chiricahua Apaches, to continue our beliefs, our ceremonies. Other faiths didn't really treat us that way; some believed we were pagans. These couldn't understand that a way of life can be like Christianity, or even deeper. They looked at us as lesser people. It's too bad that some things happen that way, but we have learned to live with it. People who count with us have encouraged us to remain the people we are.
>
> We weigh the Christian way really well and use the best of it. We try to teach our children that Christianity teaches just as well as the Indian way. However, number one

is that whether we like it or not, we have to teach background to our children . . . let them know there is a difference. We must remember to tell them that the Giver of Life, the creator, God, did not place the Apaches here with their particular language as a way for others to make a living. Who is right when God has given us our language and our particular ways and someone is asking us to leave it because it's wrong? Who is right on the face of this earth? There are so many things that you can't wear the subject out.

Berle has great regard for the Apache language and all of its inflections and flexibility: "For instance, if you are talking about a hoe, you talk about the implement, but if you want to be particular and identify the hoe, then you describe what it does. People nowadays mix English with the Apache words. Sure, it's much easier to instruct your kids in English today, but things are very descriptive in the Apache language, and once the children find out how powerful the old words are, and that there's so much detail, they become interested in it."

The first dictionary of the Apache language has finally been published, although Berle believes "there will be changes, not necessarily corrections, because it's a working dictionary. I work with it all the time. Talk about perfecting it—we'll probably be doing that all of our lives."

One of the fascinating aspects of the Apache language is its omission of certain words that other languages take for granted; for instance, the greeting "good morning." When Berle is asked how to say it in Apache, he tells people:

We don't say "good morning." And they take a second look. There are so many things understood in the Apache way that are different from the white man's world. We don't have to say "good morning" to each other. The Creator allowed us to wake up and see a good morning . . . fresh . . . with the sun coming up. The fact that it's a good morning is understood. So, if you meet your friends or pass someone, you just start talking without saying "good morning." On the other hand, if you know someone is not feeling well before bedtime, then in the morning you may ask, "How are you this morning?" Outsiders misread us and think that we are gruff, but this is how it is, and people should be able to understand other ways.

As a people, we have gotten away from our old ways a lot and practice the dominant society's customs. But it's very important for every one of us to reach back and begin with our language because that's where everything is at. Some parents who are fluent in Apache are not teaching their children the original language. But it's not just a matter of words. They must live the language at home and tell their children to pick up their socks, wash the dishes, close the screen door, etc., in the native tongue. We must return to the tribal traditions, see what our ancestors' values were, and relearn them.

My wife Lynette and I discuss the traditions and some undesirable things that have taken place, but we need to look deeper and we must remember our people's ways. Many of the customs are learned by example, by someone doing something, good or bad. You have to let your children see both, and then you point out the differences.

For instance, I've been on the church consistory, the policy-making body, better than twenty years and have seen pastors come and go. Some have been encouraged to leave, particularly one pastor who went among our people and did things that were undesirable, but his sermons were just great. The sound system in church was hooked up, and the guy who operated it recorded this pastor's sermons. My wife and I asked for these tapes, replayed them, and learned. There was so much Christian education in what he said that we chose some of these tapes for our children as they were growing up. We encouraged them to listen to the message. The pastor was just great in that regard; but on the other hand he did things that were out of place. When you weigh these two together, we didn't want him doing things out of place day to day, and he left.

We continue to say that every step of the way is very spiritual. I remember the old people at Whitetail when it was plowing time . . . harvest time. They would clear rocks out in the field and pile the rocks so they could plow and harrow and eventually plant. When they placed these rocks in a certain way, they would use the dirt for blessing, praying that every day everything would be good, as the dirt returned to mother earth . . . that it would replenish itself because there's life on earth. So this is why I continue to tell my kids that every step of our way has been very sacred and spiritual. But there are so many contradictions today that you have to work at averaging. As you mature, you begin to see how it really is and how things work. You see things differently. The main thing is to believe and that you practice your belief. You pick up some of our sacred ways in your own time and apply it because it will fit.

I asked Berle if he remembered anything special from the classroom. "Not the classroom in particular," he replied, although he remembered some things that happened outside the school building, "being that we like to identify with the outside and the free spirit and so forth that is in us from our ancestors. We were introduced to snow houses such as the Eskimos used, but we used paper boxes, and BB guns."

I recalled how angry I got when one of the boys, Ulysses Chee, shot my dog with his BB gun. To this Berle said, "Some kids wanted to see how someone else [me] reacted to ownership. They were just testing and checking, not really in a mean way, but learning about other people."

I asked Berle what happened to all the tools I bought using the candy and soda pop money I accumulated during the times I showed movies at the school. He answered, "Well, they just got pilfered by someone who knew about them, that they were valuable. A lesser person. That's one of the things you learn to be on guard against. Even today we have experiences that require caution. For instance, my wife and I don't care to shop in Ruidoso. We'll go there to pick up a quick bottle of milk or something like that, but otherwise we don't shop there because we see an attitude toward us. We prefer not to face it, so we go thirty-six miles toward Alamogordo where there are more shops and we feel we are treated fairly. That's how it is. You just learn throughout life to be on guard."

Lynette Kazhe Kanseah spoke next: "I think the Chiricahua are really smart. In one way they knew they were defeated, but that was according to the standard of the white man. The Chiricahuas have never really been defeated or we wouldn't be sitting here today with the spirit we have. It's been carried on from way back. We made it full circle. We were smart enough to know when to stop fighting and when to get along and survive. I get revenge in little ways. When a white person makes a mistake, I look at them and ask myself, how can they be so stupid? They see it coming and they still do it. It's just those little things that happen day by day."

Berle brought the topic back around to traditions:

> When I was quite small, my grandfather was reading my Sunday school paper. He had learned to read as a prisoner of war attending school in Carlisle, Pennsylvania, but his eyesight was failing at the time. He gradually began to tell one of the Sunday school stories. My aunt said, "This story isn't from the Bible, it's from your grandfather's old people." There were so many stories my grandfather knew but I didn't hear anymore. I could kick myself that I didn't ask, and just sort of took some of those things for granted. It makes me try harder to maintain my own identity. God has given us all that. It's not too late to collect some of the stories, but none are being collected, to my knowledge. We should think about using a tape recorder, especially for the stories about our medicine.
>
> I remember during my first years on the Tribal Council, people used to say, "My

uncle . . . my grandfather . . . the old people knew everything in the Indian way. And here I am, I don't know a thing." And they have hated themselves for it.

A lot of people call themselves medicine men. In all of the families there probably were people like that, someone who had a gift for healing. The medicines were handed down generation after generation, and some are still here today. There are still some who have this gift. Charley Smith has talked about it. . . . Asa Daklugie . . . Eugene Chihuahua. Some have written these things. But you read and you wonder about putting it on paper, but on the other hand we are losing the knowledge. We're not tending to it.

Many people want to come on the reservation for a month, talk to us, and go away thinking they are experts. Then there are people who have come here and blundered about in the Apache way. They were accepted quickly, and they learned about the Apaches and how they are. They appreciate and come back. They remember words in the old language. I think probably they are very special. Maybe we're a blessing to each other. It's difficult for us when people use us, when even those you count on take advantage and you are still trusting. Then you kick yourself and say "never again!" But at the same time you see a way that you can save some history for the kids. For myself, I say "shut it off here. Don't tell any more. Period."

Lynette differed: "Being a teacher I want to open up more. Berle is more reserved about things, but he has deeper feelings about what we're discussing. We both agree that we are losing a lot, probably have already, but we still want to save it somehow and it's not by letting everybody know."

Berle was especially insulted by an occurrence that took place "about the time I was getting out of high school. Some Indian medicines were taken into laboratories and experimented with. The scientists found that the medicine was detrimental to certain parts of the body. But it's healing for us, and there's no way it can be healing for us without being used in the sacred manner. The instructions for our use of the medicine was given to us through our language, and that is our identity. Our language is sacred. I grew up knowing that you don't change the language when it's handed down, but today some of the language is changing . . . which means that we're losing it. And then its sacredness becomes questionable. And then what? But down deep, we have to have faith."

Lynette added, "Two of our four children participate in the old ceremonies. They have made that choice, and I think they are our guarantee for our family. In some ways they probably know more than I do. I have written a few things down. Almost like a diary, and it's only for me. A few times I have taken this book out and read something to Berle, just to keep our minds fresh. Someday when I'm gone, the kids will have that for whatever it's worth. Just to know that this or that has happened, and certain things are the way of the people. Maybe something will come up [in their lives] that is similar and my writing might be a guide."

In discussing the children and grandchildren, Berle concluded:

> We just took our grandson home a little while ago, the son of our eldest boy. He's our first grandchild, two years old. Once our children were grown and there weren't any grandchildren, Lynette and I did everything together. Then our grandson came along. We love him, he's everything to us, but physically we need to readjust. We used to say that we missed our babies when our kids were all grown, but now we have to learn to do it all over again. This boy is just like his dad was when he was a baby. The same thing all over. Kids have to find out for themselves what their parents know is going to take place. What's happening right now is that the kids think we're old fuddy-duddies. But grandchildren are a lot of fun. It does take some work and it's like my father said, "You put your head down and work. If anyone wants to pat you on the back . . . fine . . . but you do the best you can. Never quit. "Yes, it takes work and takes some time, but that's what it's all about. So we're constantly busy, just trying to keep up."[7]

Chapter 7
Leaving Whitetail

Talking with the kids and Dorcie brought back bittersweet memories. I recall that marching side by side with the happiness I experienced at Whitetail was the thought that I would someday have to leave the place and the people I had come to love. As Doris and I finished our second year there, our feelings were mixed and confused. Both of us had grown to love the environment, the Chiricahuas, and the wonderful peace of isolation. But I was becoming more and more aware that I had neither the training nor the ability to impart wisdom to these kids. I felt that I was failing them and their parents and grandparents. In the process of my self-examination, I became convinced that I was not cut out to be a grade school teacher. I had taken a risk going to the top of that mountain, but, then, so had the BIA in sending me there.

I applied for a teaching position at one of the BIA boarding schools that taught eighth grade students and higher, where I thought I would be more comfortable, but nothing came of it. Many day-school teachers wanted to move to boarding schools in the more urban areas, so there was not the pressing shortage that there was in the community day schools like Whitetail. Finally, after talking with Lonnie Hardin, I decided to leave at the end of my term and try a year of graduate school in the field of audiovisual aids. During my stay at Whitetail I had persuaded myself that such aids could add a great deal to education, no matter what the culture of the children being taught.

My teaching contract was for a twelve-month year, not nine months as in some other educational systems, but there were no classes during the summer, so my duties were minimal. Doris and I used that last summer to organize our few possessions and say our good-byes. I cleaned my classroom for the last time in preparation for the next teacher, leaving behind the wire recorder that I had bought for the school so the children could hear themselves talk. I hoped this would improve their language skills. I also left a number of tools for the people to use—the same tools that were later stolen. The last walk through my classroom was nearly as frightening as the first one; in both cases I was stepping into a strange new world with no knowledge of what the future would bring.

Most of the Chiricahua kids and their parents trickled in during those last summer months to say their good-byes. Leroy and Hugh were the only members of the Coonie family who came to the house, but then I never really expected others to come. There was no big farewell celebration—that is not the Chiricahua way. I believe some of the older folks felt I was deserting them, although no one said so. I recall only one person saying something like, "Here only two years and you're leaving already? Don't you like us?" I couldn't find the words to tell him what I felt in my heart.

It was a melancholy day when we loaded the little trailer we had bought in Ruidoso and hooked it up to our Chrysler Windsor. No Chiricahuas were visible, but I had a feeling they were watching us. Then we drove away, trying not to look back, each carrying a real sense of loss. The farther the car rolled down out of those spectacular hills and across the flat barren plains and prairies where Doris and I had literally grown up, the more we missed the beautiful mountains and their courageous inhabitants. It felt like leaving home for the first time. Initially we kept up correspondence with Dorcie Kazhe and Father Marcian, but we lost touch with Dorcie after about five years. We eventually stopped sending Christmas cards to the Hardins, but Father Marcian continued to write every year, long after he left Mescalero, right up until his death.

After visiting with us on the reservation, my folks liked New Mexico so much that they decided to move there. A year after we left Whitetail, my father took a job at Los Alamos, far north of the reservation. For ten more years, until their deaths, we stopped to visit them there, although we never made it back to the reservation . . . except once. I made a very quick stop on my way back from a Synod meeting in El Paso during the early 1980s. A wedding reception was in progress at the Dutch Reformed Church and I poked my head in. I didn't recognize anyone, but with characteristic Apache hospitality those inside encouraged me to sit down and join them for the feast. A heavyset cook in her forties thought she recognized me and said, "I bet you don't remember me. I was one of your pupils at Whitetail." She was right. I didn't recall her name and still don't.

While I was there I took a quick drive up to Whitetail. The school was deserted, and only one home in the community looked occupied. I believe it was Hugh Coonie's place. Everyone else was gone.

Reflections from the Reverend Robert Ove

In earlier times, peace and quiet prevailed on the reservation, but on this visit I heard country and western music emanating from passing vehicles, and even the most modest home had a television set blaring away, with commercial demands to "rush right down to your neighborhood store and...." Chiricahua Apache children are absorbing the white man's culture, eating the white man's food, and buying the white man's luxuries; in the process they are losing their own culture, language, and identity. I wonder if Apaches like Berle and Lynette Kanseah can preserve the spirit of this once-proud people, or whether all will one day dissolve into the anonymity of the American melting pot. There is a secrecy about Apache ways that may prove their undoing. It is as though sharing customs and their meaning with non-Indians will somehow taint the old ways. I urged Berle and Lynette to write down some of their traditions and legends before these fade from memory. I know they have tried, but the dominant culture's emphasis on busy-ness has infected their lives, as well.

My experience with the Apaches changed the solid assurance of my early years forever. Living in their culture, even for a brief two years, opened up a multitude of insights into my own "white" culture. My old preconceptions were dashed. The things I had learned about Indians in classrooms and movie theaters were so far from the reality I experienced that I felt I could never again accept anything I read or heard about Indians at face value. I never reached a point where I wanted to dump all my values and trade them for Apache values, but I developed then, and still possess, a strong feeling that both cultures can learn from each other. I lost completely the old "superiority" attitude that white people are the only ones who have anything worthwhile to pass on.

I believe the main reason that the Apaches accepted me is that they felt my love and growing respect for them. I listened to their stories with genuine interest. I was concerned about the sick and troubled. I was nonjudgmental about most of the differences in our customs. They knew I cared about them, and they reciprocated. They were friendly to me—even some of those who had experienced firsthand the white man's "justice"—because I chose to live among them. I was vulnerable. I was totally at their mercy in one respect, and they could see that I trusted them. Perhaps they saw me as a bridge to the future, to more peaceful relations, and wanted to see their children freed of the burden of distrust and hatred that they had endured for so long.

At least one thing remains as it was: the beautiful hills and trees and mountains will always surround Whitetail, long after human beings have turned to dust. Whitetail is still God's country, and it remains home to the spirits of the Chiricahuas who survived three decades of incarceration as prisoners of war. I pray that this place will always be home to the Chiricahua Apaches, and to others who have been blessed by its spirituality. As Henrietta is, as I was and still am nearly half a century later.

Afterthoughts from Henrietta Stockel

Bob Ove's two years at Whitetail occurred during a much more innocent time in America, when attitudes toward Native Americans were not as sophisticated or as sensitive as they are today. Ove's recollections of Whitetail and the Chiricahua Apaches document a time and place—it is the story not only of people but of himself as a decent, well-meaning, thoughtful, but sadly unprepared young teacher in an alien and often difficult environment. His memories, often humorous, describe the pain and confusion of not fitting in and occasionally reveal the pathos of his situation. Never is there an indication of malice. Ove's actions within the circumstances of life on the Mescalero Apache Reservation were not only appropriate for the time, but were compassionate, curious, and reflective. Conveying his experiences at this period of his life benefits from maturity and perspective. He aged considerably, became a minister and a father, divorced and then remarried, and moved around the country to preach in various towns and cities. The Chiricahua children he taught are now adults themselves; they have raised families, struggled to earn a living, buried their loved ones, and watched the traditional ways of their ancestors fade into history. For example, the ancient Apache belief system that relied on one's word as one's bond no longer exists. These days the need for more formal assurances is part of modern reservation life at Mescalero; paying bills on time has replaced promises.

If cultural change occurs in response to the impact of external environmental pressures, it logically follows that the people must change also.

But is that true of a place as well? Whitetail, for example, is now uninhabited, the old wooden structures that sheltered the people and their animals are sinking into the dark earth, and the wind swirls freely in the tall pines, unimpeded. However, at Whitetail what remains unaffected by outside forces is the power of the place, its spirit. Through the years, regardless of the varying degrees of acculturation and assimilation that occurred among Chiricahuas, Whitetail's enduring hold on all who love the place did not change. Just ask Vernon Simmons, or Berle and Lynette Kanseah, for example. They will tell you that Whitetail's spirit is powerful medicine. Still today it floats through the air and embraces, envelops, and caresses everyone's memories. It fills the palpable silence up there in that sacred place, much as children's giggles once did, much as young lovers' whispers once did, and much as old timers' tales once did. And when it takes a notion, this living spirit calls its people home, no matter where they are. It stretched its arms out to Bob Ove in Cheyenne, Wyoming, then drifted south to twenty miles upriver from Albuquerque, New Mexico, and beckoned to me. The Rev and I, strangers brought to each other by Whitetail's spirit, joined together and wrote this book.

Frequently, that mysterious quintessence dips down the mountain and reminds today's senior-citizen Chiricahuas to drive up and slowly make their way along the dirt road that passes the schoolhouse, just to keep the memories alive. It speaks to certain families planning puberty ceremonies and persuades them to hold the ancient ritual on the far side of the oat field, but still in sight of the old schoolhouse. It draws medicine men to secret places among the tall pines, there to pray aloud, drum, sing, and summon power. It convinces folks way out in Oklahoma—Mildred Cleghorn, for one—to visit and point out who lived where back in the early 1950s when she worked and resided among the women of that community. And recent rumor has it that at least one modern Chiricahua family plans to return to Whitetail in the near future and live there permanently.

What a dramatic change that will be from the contemporary ways now preferred by almost everyone at Mescalero. Making a new home at Whitetail will require some radical adjustments to a less comfortable lifestyle, but Chiricahua Apaches are no strangers to adaptation. They can look over their shoulders, back in time, to identify their distant ancestors' introduction into the southwest as the first cultural change the group experienced. The arid desert and mountain climate contrasted with the cold weather of their former homelands in the north, the food supply, animals and plants, was strange, the earth's healing medicines were new to them, and the physical environment was geographically distinct from Alaska's MacKenzie River Valley. Nonetheless, the Chiricahua forebears stayed in this region and accordingly adjusted their cultural infrastructure and traditional customs.

By the time the Spanish and, later, the Anglos, appeared in Apache country, a familiar way of life had been established. Accommodation to the newcomers was at first troublesome, then terrible. The outcome, of course, was imprisonment and subsequent release, decades later, to New Mexico and Oklahoma. Incarceration forced the people to conform to the ways of their captors, for to resist, in the Chiricahua view, was to die. Eve Ball's record of oral history reveals that during the long train ride from Arizona east to Fort Marion, Florida, soldiers guarding the prisoners taunted them with gestures such as running their fingers across their necks, indicating to the Apaches that they would have their throats cut. Jasper Kanseah remembered, "When they put us on that train at [Fort] Bowie, nobody thought that we'd get far before they'd stop and kill us,"[1] Young Kanseah's fears were not without foundation. United States government records show that just three weeks earlier, in a series of telegrams anticipating the capitulation of Geronimo's group, President Grover Cleveland, Acting Secretary of War R. C. Drum, and Gen. Nelson A. Miles had debated the group's destiny. President Cleveland said he hoped "nothing will be done with Geronimo which will prevent our treating him as a prisoner of war, if we cannot hang him, which I would much prefer."[2] No wonder the appearance of total compliance by the prisoners occurred immediately and became more and more of an automatic action as time passed.

At the end of the period of confinement, some degree of acculturation and assimilation had taken place. Chiricahua children had been educated in government boarding schools, and many of their parents had been successfully proselytized by missionaries from the Dutch Reformed Church of America. Absorption into the dominant society seemed to be a reality, particularly for those Apaches who remained in Oklahoma.

But most of the families who settled at Whitetail refused to mingle very much with white people or even with the other Apache groups—the Mescaleros and the Lipans—living on the reservation. For decades the kids did not go to public schools in surrounding towns, thus preserving the use of the Apache language. Traditional rituals had been kept alive in the hearts and minds of the folks throughout their long imprisonment; puberty ceremonies continued and ancient customs, such as reliance on creation myths to guide behavior, remained strong. In due time, however, socializing occurred with the other two reservation communities, but not yet with Hispanic and Anglo residents of the nearby towns. In the early to mid-1950s, when most of the Whitetail residents relocated closer to the center of Mescalero, the Chiricahuas entered the local mainstream, so to speak. In public schools off the reservation, children mixed with other kids from Ruidoso and Tularosa. The Apache language, still spoken at home, was replaced with English during outside activities, and advertising campaigns in newspapers, magazines, and on the radio convinced the people that the outside culture's modern amenities were most desirable. Eve Ball told me that in the early 1950s she saw the Apaches trudging into town to wash their clothes at the local "washeteria." Many Apaches did not own cars yet and still rode in buggies drawn by horses. Others walked for lack of any transportation, but the process of modernization could not be denied. Almost fifty years later most homes on the reservation have the accouterments of contemporary life, including washers and dryers, television sets, satellite dishes, VCRs, trucks, vans, and other vehicles.

At the 1996 puberty ceremony, one traditional Apache man hoisted a camcorder on his shoulder, aimed the lens at one of the maidens, and produced a video for her family. However, certain traditional pursuits still live among Chiricahuas old and young.

Each year more and more girls participate in the puberty ceremony, whether the rituals are held collectively in public, as on the Fourth of July weekend, or privately in more secluded areas of the reservation. Mountain Spirit dance groups continue to form, and boys still act as clowns and apprentices to the dancers. The ancient Apache war dance has been recreated and performed. At least two young Chiricahua Apache medicine men conduct ages-old ceremonies with knowledge passed on to them by the elders; one has recently performed a traditional wedding ceremony. The Apache language is taught in the reservation's elementary school classrooms.

Still, conflicts remain. Berle and Lynette Kanseah worry about losing their traditional heritage and cannot decide whether to bring outsiders into their circle and reveal their rich legacy or to keep inside their culture the customs that have endured throughout time. If the former, who will it be? How will it be handled? What is the potential for misuse? If the latter, will it be passed on accurately? And for how long? Will anyone break the chain?

The health history of the Chiricahuas, for example, had never been documented in written form until my book, *Survival of the Spirit,* was published. Many Apaches knew a little something of the topic, but the full story had not been made public, because the people themselves were unaware of many of the details. Now the information has been printed and will not be lost to history.

Part of the tragic story includes descriptions of ancient remedies for ailments that affected the Chiricahuas long before newcomers appeared in Apache country. Most of those treatments would not even be considered today, for most ailing Chiricahuas seek help at the Indian Health Service Hospital or from private physicians. Very few, if any, rely solely on traditional plant medicines or on the healing ceremonies conducted by medicine men and women. Nonetheless, certain people on the reservation, mainly elders, believe these old ways can supplement modern cures, and they take advantage of them. Afflictions of alcoholism, diabetes, and violence affect the Chiricahuas today, but medical and social demons of one kind or another have always plagued the people before incarceration, alcohol and violence were already part of their lives, and contagious diseases also caused great distress.

Early missionaries succeeded in their efforts, for Catholicism and Protestantism are the major Christian religions on the reservation today. The old ways of worship are still practiced by some, however, and there appears to be no antagonism toward this. Wendell Chino, the chairman of the Mescalero Apaches (which includes all three reservation groups), has held his position for decades; he is an ordained minister of the Dutch Reformed Church, but he does not preach. Economic development efforts, such as Casino Apache and a planned nuclear waste repository, have been quite successful yet controversial, but was there ever a time when Chiricahua endeavors of any sort did not cause contention?

The history of this great people and their external relations has always been the stuff of legends, and the passage of time has not dimmed that trait. Yes, certainly, the outside culture has had an impact and has caused many changes, but the traditional vitality—the power and strength—of the Chiricahuas has refused to surrender. Whether jailers punish them with imprisonment as in the past, or current detractors lambaste them in the news media for their business enterprises, the mighty Chiricahua Apache spirit, so evident at Whitetail and in the bones and the blood of the people, can neither be totally captured nor totally compromised.

"We're not like the other groups," said Kathleen Kanseah, great-granddaughter of the warrior Clee-neh. "We're Chiricahuas, and we will never give in, not as long as one drop of Apache blood flows in our veins."[3]

Notes

Preface

1. Quoted in Angie Debo, *Geronimo: The Man, His Time, His Place*, p. 259.
2. H. Henrietta Stockel, *Survival of the Spirit: Chiricahua Apaches in Captivity*, pp. 131–32.
3. Soon after Geronimo died on February 17, 1909, the United States government showed interest in releasing the Chiricahua Apache prisoners of war from Fort Sill, Oklahoma, by beginning bureaucratic processes that lasted inordinately long—four years. Interagency turf wars between the Departments of War and Interior caused the delays until, at long last, Interior compromised: the Chiricahuas would not be allotted land at Fort Sill, as they had originally proposed. Instead, the majority of the prisoners would be transferred to the Mescalero Apache Reservation in south-central New Mexico. Initially, on June 26, 1909, the United States Indian Inspector James McLaughlin met with a committee of Mescaleros to hear their comments, most quite favorable about the relocation. James A. Carroll, the Mescalero Agency Superintendent, concurred. Details about this meeting can be found in a document entitled "Minutes of Conference Held at the Mescalero Agency, New Mexico, June 26, 1909, by James McLaughlin, US Indian Inspector, with the Mesclaero Apaches with Reference to the removal of the Fort Sill Apaches to the Mescalero Reservation, Mescalero Agency, New Mexico, June 26, 1909," File 53 119-09-123 Kiowa, Part I, Central Files, 1907–39, Bureau of Indian Affairs, RG 75, Natural Resources Branch, Civil Archives, NARS. By June 30, 1909, McLaughlin had submitted his report recommending transfer to the Secretary of the Interior.

   Although many Chiricahuas wanted to live at Mescalero, a sizable number did not, and for a valid reason. When they were moved from the prison site at Mount Vernon, Alabama, to Fort Sill, in October, 1894, they were promised by the government that the field artillery post would be their permanent home. Having lived at Fort Sill for nearly twenty years, these Apaches indicated in public and private conversations that they preferred to stay exactly where they were. But, the government had other plans for the military installation. On September 21, 1911, a conference was held at Fort Sill with the Apache leaders. Colonel Hugh L. Scott represented the administration and stated that there had been a misunderstanding—Fort Sill had never been promised in perpetuity to the prisoners. Rather, he said, it was only meant to be a temporary home until other arrangements could be made. Furthermore, Scott announced, no Apache would be freed from the status of prisoner of war until he/she left Fort Sill. Author John J. Turcheneske, in "'It Is Right That They Should Set Us Free:' The Role of the War and Interior Departments," *Red River Valley Historical Review* 4 (Summer, 1979): 13, reports that Talbot Goody, one of the leaders responded bitterly to Scott by saying there was "only one way out"—either move to Mescalero and become free or remain as prisoners of war at Fort Sill.

The Apaches voted. One hundred sixty-three chose Mescalero [the numbers vary according to document]; eighty-eight preferred to stay in Oklahoma. For the latter, allotments of land near Fort Sill belonging to deceased Kiowas and Comanches could be purchased from their families for $2,000 to $3,000 each. After years of political resistance from ranching and farming interests in New Mexico who wanted the reservation land to graze their cattle, in late December, 1912, Interior Secretary Walter L. Fisher officially requested a sum of $300,000 from Congress for both projects—$221,500 to be allocated for the needs of those remaining in Oklahoma and $78,500 for those moving to Mescalero. On Wednesday, April 2, 1913, a Rock Island special train left the Fort Sill depot bound for Tularosa, New Mexico, just south of the Mescalero Apache Reservation. On Friday morning, April 4, a delegation of Mescaleros welcomed the detraining Chiricahuas and escorted them to the reservation. In a prior meeting with the Mescaleros, Chiricahua leader Asa Daklugie had obtained their permission to have his group relocated. In return, he promised the Mescaleros that they could share in the profits of the Chiricahuas' cattle herd, being run at Fort Sill by the prisoners. An area called Whitetail, a narrow, eight-mile-long valley over seven thousand feet in elevation, was the only area on the reservation then unoccupied and fit for cattle herds.

4. Stockel, *Women of the Apache Nation: Voices of Truth,* pp. 73–74.
5. Ibid., p. 37.

Introduction

1. Geronimo was born into the Bedonkohe band of Apaches and was not a true Chiricahua. For a fuller explanation, see Stockel, *Survival of the Spirit,* p. 3.
2. Stockel, *Survival of the Spirit,* pp. 116–17. An entire chapter of this book is devoted to the startling truth about the Chiricahua children's experiences at Carlisle. The author has compiled a list from various obscure sources of the names of the children who perished while held at this institution. She describes the bureaucratic neglect that led to an ever increasing number of sick and dying youngsters, many of whom, when terminally ill, were placed on trains and sent back to the prisoner of war camp to die.
3. Ibid., p. 117.
4. Eve Ball with Nora Henn and Lynda Sanchez, *Indeh: An Apache Odyssey,* p. 149.
5. *Carlisle Indian School Catalog,* p. 10. This complete catalog is quite informative and describes in great detail all of the "opportunities" available to students.

Chapter 1. Remembering Whitetail

1. Bears hold no positive significance for the Chiricahua Apaches, as they do for many other Native American groups. On the contrary, many negative connotations swirl around the subject, and the people judiciously avoid contact with or even the mention of bears. Terrible sickness is thought to be the result of coming across one, even accidently. The ailment(s) are very difficult to cure unless the victim enlists the services of a shaman skilled in treating bear encounters.
2. The Chiricahua Apaches' relations with the U.S. government have been disastrous for them. See Stockel, *Survival of the Spirit,* and Ball, *Indeh,* for the Chiricahua Apache point of view.
3. Brown, correspondence with Stockel, November 8, 1992. For a detailed description of the catastrophes that occurred among the Chiricahuas in captivity, see Stockel, *Survival of the Spirit.*
4. At the same time Bob Ove was teaching at Whitetail, a diminutive southerner named Eve Ball lived in Ruidoso, New Mexico, a town that abuts the Mescalero Apache Reservation. Ball had come several years earlier to the area as a schoolteacher and became acquainted with these same Chiricahua Apaches. Through her gentle ways, and with great persistence and kindness, she convinced some of the sons and daughters of the great Apache leaders, including Asa Daklugie and Eugene Chihuahua, to tell their stories to her. After thirty years Ball concluded her interviews and writings and published *Indeh: An Apache Odyssey.* It is unusual that the Chiricahuas were simultaneously confiding in Ove and Ball. Mrs. Ball passed away at the age of ninety-four on December 24, 1984. We do not know if she knew of Ove's work at Whitetail, but he was told about her and knew that the Chiricahuas affectionately called her "the white lady of Ruidoso" and "the old lady with many stories."

Chapter 2. The Whitetail Day School

1. Some of the elders watching their grandchildren take part in the presentation may have recalled another time, way back in the distant Christmas season of 1889 when they, as the youngest prisoners of war, first celebrated the holiday. There were seven boys over the age of twelve, four girls over twelve, sixty-seven boys under twelve, and fifty-eight girls under twelve in the Mount Vernon, Alabama, prison camp.

   Two women missionaries from the Dutch Reformed Church, Vincentine T. Booth and Marion E. Stephens, taught the children then in a one-room building furnished by the government. The teachers had a bit of trouble maintaining order at first, and learning was at a minimum. When Geronimo heard about it, however, the problem was soon solved. He went out and broke a switch off a nearby tree and, uninvited, patrolled the aisles of the classroom, ready to swat any disobedient or troublesome student.

   In this Alabama schoolhouse, located on what is now an overgrown field on the grounds of a state mental institution, the Apaches' first Christmas festivities were held. Author Woody Skinner described the event in *The Apache Rock Crumbles,* pp. 237–38. Many of the administrative personnel at the prison camp worked with full hearts to ensure that the Apache children had a happy time. Preparations began in November when the teachers started informing their students about the religious history of the holy day. Wives of military personnel in charge of the prison camp donated time and money for the secular side of the event. A former Army officer and his wife, reassigned to Massachusetts, sent four hundred gold and silver cornucopias.

After breakfast on Christmas Eve morning, the children stood outside the school door, kept out by locked doors, their view to the inside blocked by newspapers covering the windows. It was a long day for them, but as soon as dark fell, candles on the tree inside were lighted and the youngsters were permitted to enter. The tree was a holly, covered with red berries, with a white and silver angel perched on the tallest branch. Brightly wrapped presents for the Apache children were all around. Santa Claus, in the person of white interpreter George Wratten, wore a black fur cap, a white cotton beard, and his own mustache. He greeted the children in their own language, distributed bags of candy, and acknowledged with Apache witticisms the two curious Apache adults who had crept into the room—Geronimo and Chief Naiche. After the small gifts were distributed, the children were permitted to open other presents that had been waiting under the tree for them. Each wide-eyed child received a spinning top, a bag of marbles, a pencil, a slate, a horn, and a picture book.

Chapter 3. If Only I Had Known . . .

1. Stockel, *Women of the Apache Nation*, p. 35.
2. Ibid., p. 69.
3. Stockel, *Survival of the Spirit*, p. 3.
4. Morris E. Opler, "Chiricahua Apache," *Handbook of North American Indians*, vol. 10, p. 401.
5. William B. Griffen, *Apaches at War and Peace: The Janos Presidio, 1750–1858*, p. 5.
6. Max Moorhead, *The Apache Frontier: Jacobo Ugarte and Spanish-Indian Relations in Northern New Spain, 1769–1791*, p. 4.
7. Stockel, *Survival of the Spirit*, p. 77.
8. Ball, *Indeh*, p. 133.
9. Ibid., p. 131.
10. Quoted in Britton Davis, *The Truth about Geronimo*, pp. 225–26.
11. U.S. Senate, Exec. Doc. 117 (49-2), p. 29.
12. U.S. Senate, Exec. Doc. 35 (51-1), p. 37.

Chapter 4. The Old Timers at Whitetail

1. Debo, *Geronimo*, pp. 76–77. Ishton's child was Asa Daklugie.
2. Gillett Griswold, "The Fort Sill Apaches: Their Vital Statistics, Tribal Origins, Antecedents," p. 42, U.S. Army and Missile Center Museum Archives, Fort Sill, Okla., 1970. Griswold was a director of the museum at Fort Sill. His "Vital Statistics" is the only information of its kind available on the genealogy of the Chiricahua Apaches.
3. Ball, *Indeh*, pp. 262–63.
4. Dorothy Emerson, *Among the Mescalero Apaches: The Story of Father Albert Braun, OFM,*

p. 41. There is a wonderful photograph of the Robert Geronimo wedding party on p. 40. Everyone looks morose, especially the bride.
5. I do not know what became of Juanita. See Griswold, "Vital Statistics," pp. 44–45.
6. Ball, *Indeh*, pp. 62–63. It was always a puzzle to me that Daklugie didn't know that Robert was a close relative before he and Maude were married. Everyone on the reservation knew that Robert was Geronimo's son and that Daklugie and Geronimo were kin. But living with the Chiricahuas, I learned that there are some things that will never be explained, and this is one of them.
7. Ibid., p. 263n.
8. Griswold, "Vital Statistics," p. 28.
9. Interviews with Dorcie Kazhe, July and August 1993.
10. For a complete description of the children's years in this institution and the diseases they suffered, see Stockel, *Survival of the Spirit,* pp. 113–36.
11. Ball, conversation with Stockel, May, 1982.
12. This is an example of the Apache kinship system. Eliza Coonie was indeed Dahteste's stepdaughter, but she was known in Whitetail as her niece.
13. At least one bald-headed and white-wisped Apache with steel-blue eyes lives outside Tucson, Arizona, smack in the middle of the desert. Claiming to be a grandson of Geronimo, the old fellow resides in a structure that resembles a tar-paper shack and sells rocks and his baby picture to passing tourists. It is a C. S. Fly photo of Geronimo, Naiche, Chappo, and a young man holding a baby. The latter two have been identified by Chiricahua Apache Elbys Hugar as Perico, a warrior, and his baby daughter. However, the old man's misidentification should in no way mar his credibility. He closely resembles Geronimo, with the exception of his bald pate and eyes, and for a two-dollar contribution that affirms his validity he will tell family stories and Apache war tales. He is convincing, but one wonders.

Inside the shack are photos of him standing beside various celebrities who have stopped by to see for themselves. One rickety bed and a few pots and pans are scattered about. His source of water is unknown, but he seems to do very well and to enjoy his occupation.
14. Ball, *Indeh,* pp. 213–15.
15. Ball, conversation with Stockel, May, 1982.

Chapter 5. Religion, Other White Folks, and Chiricahua Apache Justice
1. Stockel, *Women of the Apache Nation,* pp. 96–97.
2. Grenville Goodwin, "White Mountain Apache Religion," *American Anthropologist* 40 (1938): 26–27. Although Goodwin's description of White Painted Woman refers directly to the White Mountain Apaches' deity, the Chiricahuas' beliefs are similar.
3. Thomas E. Mails, *The People Called Apache,* p. 76.
4. S. M. Barrett, *Geronimo: His Own Story,* pp. 59–64.
5. Ibid, pp. 59–64.
6. Morris E. Opler, *Myths and Tales of the Chiricahua Apache Indians,* p. 15.
7. For detailed descriptions of the two rites, see Stockel, *Women of the Apache Nation,* pp.

5–12, 113–14, 155–64; and Stockel, *Survival of the Spirit*, pp. 89–90. The dance was forbidden in captivity because it was thought that the dancers' masks were fertile breeding grounds for the tuberculosis bacilli. Since the masks were shared by three or more dancers, they may have helped to spread the disease throughout the prison camps. The next record of the dance of the Mountain Spirits is a rare photograph taken of several children, probably at Fort Sill, dressed as dancers (see Stockel, *Survival of the Spirit*, p. 222). It is most unusual for children to act as dancers; ordinarily only a young boy portrays the clown and twirls around behind the adult male dancers. Disease may have so thoroughly decimated the dancers that the Chiricahuas decided to initiate boys in the hope that they would live long enough to become adults and represent Mountain Spirits in the dance.

8. Ball, *Indeh*, pp. 102–104, 263–66.
9. The only time I ever questioned Charley's expertise was when he brought his daughter to the teacherage one night complaining that she had some strange malady unfamiliar to him, and that she needed a medical doctor right away. Even I could tell that she was in the last stages of pregnancy. We put her in the school bus and rushed her down the mountain to the hospital at Mescalero, where her "strange illness" was promptly treated.
10. Dan L. Thrapp, *Encyclopedia of Frontier Biography*, vol. 1, p. 287. Clum was a youth of only twenty-two when he was named agent, possibly as a result of a relative's influence. At that time the Dutch Reformed church was supplying agents and missionaries to some Apache groups. Clum lasted three years in the post before he quit in a huff in July, 1877. He is said to have founded the *Tombstone (Arizona) Epitaph,* one of the most popular newspapers in the West, in 1880, and to have a varied career thereafter, dying at age eighty-one of a heart attack. Clum's written memoirs, according to Thrapp, are "wildly inaccurate and while useful, must be employed with some caution...."
11. Ball, *Indeh*, p. 56. Ball's book contains many statements from Chiricahuas describing their traditional religion. In particular, pages 56–65 address the Apache concept of one God, the ways of worship, spiritual taboos, descriptions of ceremonies, the use of pollen in rituals, and witchcraft.
12. This tale was reiterated to Ove in correspondence with Pastor Reuben TenHaken's wife, Bernice, who quoted Belle Kazhe, a Chiricahua. Said Kazhe to TenHaken at a Thanksgiving celebration, "Our ancestors told us about a higher power—God—and said that someday a man with yellow hair, blue eyes, and a book under his arm would come and he would have the truth and we should hear and listen to his words, and that came true when the first white man (missionaries) came to our Apaches." See also Stockel, "The Lady in Blue: A Pueblo Indian Legend," p. 42. New Mexico's Pueblo Indians still tell of a mysterious lady in a blue cloak who talked with the Indians' ancestors about Jesus and Christianity long before the Spanish arrived in the early 1600s. Speaking fluently in the distinct Pueblo village dialects, this woman was so convincing that when the priests and conquistadors appeared, the Indians' first request was for baptism as it had been described to their ancestors by the visitor.
13. Stockel, *Survival of the Spirit*, p. 117.

14. Sister Juanita, conversation with Stockel, August, 1993.
15. Lonnie told me that he met Beulah in college and that they dated for about a week before they were engaged. It was another week before they were married. The union lasted until her death just a few years ago. Lonnie, now in his eighties, has remarried.
16. Donald E. Worcester, "Early Spanish Accounts of the Apache Indians," p. 310; Gordon C. Baldwin's *The Apache Indians: Raiders of the Southwest,* p. 147, shows a photo of Cut Nose, a Chiricahua woman who paid the price for her actions. She later became a spy for the army against her own people. Many authors have written about the high moral standards of the Chiricahuas, including their prohibition against lying, their commendable treatment of children, and their respect for elders. Many of the traditional traits are still observed today.
17. Today the U.S. Army routinely tests its weapons on the firing range at White Sands, a barren strip of gypsum and desert vegetation that has played an important role in American military history. Trinity Site, a hundred or so miles to the north, is where the atom bomb was tested on July 16, 1945.

Chapter 6. Talks with the Kids and the Cook

1. Interview with Vernon Simmons, August 1993. Vernon's Comanche grandmother told him that her grandfather had had five wives until the white men told him that he had to get rid of all but one. He did not want to, but apparently he was forced to abandon four women. Grandmother Hernannie also told Vernon that she had an Indian name but when she was taken to the Fort Sill, Oklahoma, Indian School, she was told never to use it. She stayed at the school for three days, until her father returned to the tribe from a hunting expedition and learned of his daughter's whereabouts. Then the Comanche man took his gun and rode his horse to the school. "I come after my daughter," he said. "She don't belong here." The soldiers said she had to stay or he would go to jail, so Hernannie's father forced a showdown. He cocked his gun and aimed it, telling the military man to make up his mind. The Comanche man was told to put his gun down and take his daughter back to the tribe. "She only went to school for three days," Vernon said.
2. The name of the peaks in Dahteste's description is probably Dos Cabezas. The Chiricahuas of old did not assign place names but rather remembered geographical locations and their specific meanings. That became clear when we asked contemporary descendants if they knew the names of the peaks. None did, but all knew where they were. In former times, the sight of these two peaks probably indicated to Cochise's band that they were nearing the safety of his stronghold.
3. Opler, *Myths and Tales,* p. 15.
4. Stockel, *Survival of the Spirit,* p. 16. Another tale of an owl concerns an old woman, a survivor of the prisoner-of-war years who was brushing her long hair in the Oklahoma sunshine and humming a pleasant tune. Suddenly her song turned to screams. An owl had landed on her head and refused to leave, despite the blows she frantically rained on it with her hairbrush. Not too long after that the old woman died, ostensibly of unknown causes, but the reason for her death was no mystery to the Chiricahuas. They knew the owl was responsible.

5. Interviews with Dorcie Kazhe, July and August 1993. Dorcie's mother-in-law was Emma Toklanni Kazhe, the daughter of Rogers Toklanni and Siki. Rogers Toklanni was a Warm Springs Apache who is said to have held the record for the longest stint as a United States Army scout. He was imprisoned nonetheless, along with his wife, Siki, the daughter of Warm Springs Apache chief Loco. Siki escaped death at the massacre of Chief Victorio and his people at Tres Castillos but was taken captive by the Mexicans and sold into slavery in Mexico City. Three years later she and two other women fled. Carrying only one knife and one blanket, they found their way back home, a journey of nearly a thousand miles that has been described in great detail in Eve Ball's *In the Days of Victorio: Recollections of a Warm Springs Apache*, pp. 168–74.
6. More information about traditional customs can be found in Stockel, *Women of the Apache Nation*.
7. Interviews with Berle and Lynette Kanseah, July 3, 1992, and July and August 1993.

Chapter 7. Leaving Whitetail

1. Ball, *Indeh*, p. 131.
2. Stockel, *Survival of the Spirit*, p. 95.
3. Conversation with K. Kanseah, October 12, 1996.

Bibliography

Books and Articles

Ball, Eve. *In the Days of Victorio: Recollections of a Warm Springs Apache.* Tucson: University of Arizona Press, 1970.

Ball, Eve with Nora Henn and Lynda Sanchez. *Indeh: An Apache Odyssey.* Provo: Brigham Young University, 1980.

Baldwin, Gordon C. *The Apache Indians: Raiders of the Southwest.* New York: Four Winds Press, 1978.

Barrett, S. M. *Geronimo: His Own Story.* New York: Ballantine Books, 1971.

Davis, Britton. *The Truth about Geronimo.* Lincoln: University of Nebraska Press, 1929.

Debo, Angie. *Geronimo: The Man, His Time, His Place.* Norman: University of Oklahoma Press, 1976.

Emerson, Dorothy. *Among the Mescalero Apaches: The Story of Father Albert Braun, OFM.* Tucson: University of Arizona Press, 1973.

Goodwin, Grenville. "White Mountain Apache Religion." *American Anthropologist* 40 (1938): 24–37.

Griffen, William B. *Apaches at War and Peace: The Janos Presidio, 1750–1858.* Albuquerque: University of New Mexico Press, 1988.

Griswold, Gillett. "The Fort Sill Apaches: Their Vital Statistics, Tribal Origins, Antecedents." U.S. Army and Missile Center Museum Archives. Fort Sill, Okla., 1970.

Mails, Thomas E. *The People Called Apache.* 1st ed. Englewood Cliffs, N.J.: Prentice Hall, 1974.

Moorhead, Max. *The Apache Frontier: Jacobo Ugarte and Spanish-Indian Relations in Northern New Spain, 1769–1791.* Norman: University of Oklahoma Press, 1968.

Opler, Morris E. *Myths and Tales of the Chiricahua Apache Indians.* New York: Kraus Reprint Company, 1969.

———. "Chiricahua Apache." *Handbook of North American Indians* 10 (1938): 401–18.

Skinner, Woodward B. *The Apache Rock Crumbles: The Captivity of Geronimo's People.* Pensacola, Fla.: Skinner Publications, 1987.

Stockel, H. Henrietta. "The Lady in Blue: A Pueblo Indian Legend." *Queen of All Hearts Magazine* (September–October 1988): 42–43.

———. *Survival of the Spirit: Chiricahua Apaches in Captivity.* Reno: University of Nevada Press, 1993.

———. *Women of the Apache Nation: Voices of Truth.* Reno: University of Nevada Press, 1991.

Sweeney, Edwin. *Cochise: Chiricahua Apache Chief.* Norman: University of Oklahoma Press, 1991.

Thrapp, Dan L. *Encyclopedia of Frontier Biography,* vols. 1–4. Lincoln: University of Nebraska Press, 1988.

Worcester, Donald E. "Early Spanish Accounts of the Apache Indians." *American Anthropologist,* n.s., 43 (1941): 308–12.

Interviews, Conversations, and Correspondence

Ball, Eve. Conversation with Stockel at Ball's home, May 2, 1982.

Brown, Dee. Correspondence with Stockel, November 8, 1992.

Kanseah, Berle, and Lynette Kanseah. Interviews with Ove, July 3, 1992, July and August, 1993.

Kanseah, Kathleen. Conversation with Stockel, October 12, 1996.

Kazhe, Dorcie. Interviews with Ove, July and August, 1993.

Simmons, Vernon. Interview with Ove, August, 1993.

Sister Juanita. Conversation with Stockel at Saint Joseph's Mission on the Mescalero Apache Reservation, August, 1993.

Government Documents

United States Senate. Executive Document 35. Vol. 2686, 51st Cong., 1st sess.

———. Executive Document 117, Vol. 2358, 49th Cong., 2nd sess.

Miscellaneous

Carlisle Indian School Catalog, Carlisle, Pa.: Carlisle Indian Press, 1912.

Index

animals, birds, and wildlife at Whitetail, 13–14, 16–17, 19–20, 78, 111, 121–22, 137n 1

Baldwin, Gordon, 141n 16
Ball, Eve, 89, 137n 4, 140n 11
Blazer, Art, 95
Bucher, Father Marcian, 90–91
Bureau of Indian Affairs: lawyer visits Whitetail to discuss Chiricahua land claims at, 102; policies in the 1940s of, 6; and Ove's house at Whitetail, ix, 7–8

Carlisle Indian School: Chiricahua Apache children attend, xxix–xxx, 136n 2; history of, xxvii; outing system of, xxx, 54; tuberculosis and contagious diseases at, xxix–xxx
Chee, Hugh: death of, 73; as nephew of Cochise, 70; and polygamy, 71–72; as prisoner of war, 70; supernatural experience of, 70–71
Chihuahua, Eugene: discusses problems and housing, 59; marries three wives, 58; as prisoner of war, 58; recalled by Vernon Simmons, 106–108; sings in church, 88; travels to Mexico, 60
Chiricahua Apaches: and attitude toward education, xxvii; bears, 137n 1; burial customs of, 73–74; cards as entertainment for, xiii; ceremonies, traditional, 92, 107–108; children's education during incarceration, xxvii–xxxi; and Christianity, 120, 121, 140n 1; cradleboards, 83–84; cultural characteristics, 52, 72–74, 78; customs of, 16, 82; and diseases acquired during incarceration, and deaths, x–xi; and first exposure to Catholicism, 90; history of, 36–45; homelands of, x; kinship system of, 46–47; and living conditions at Whitetail (1913), xi; matrilocality, 116; mother-in-law avoidance, 80, 119; newspaper headlines (1880s), x; polygamy, 71–72; prisoners of war, 40–45, 135n 3; procedures leading to release of prisoners of war, 135n 3; religion, traditional, 85–86, 106–107; structures of bands, 39–40; structures of speeches, 79; warfare strategy of, 65–66; and women's roles, 53–54, 81
Cleghorn, Mildred Imach, ancestral relationship with Kathleen Kanseah, xix, 47
Clum, John, 140n 10
Coonie, Hugh: attempts salesmanship, 77; Marmaduke the horse, 78; parents of, 76; as prisoner of war, 76; and stepmother Dahteste (Old Lady Coonie), 76

Dahteste (Old Lady Coonie): as described by Elbys Hugar, 36–37; lives with niece

Dahteste (Old Lady Coonie) (*continued*) Eliza Coonie, xv; and marriage to Kuni, 76; Ove's memories of, xxvi, 76; questioned by BIA lawyer regarding land claims, 102; recalled by Vernon Simmons, 106; sent by Geronimo to initiate peace talks with U.S. Army, xv, xxvii; stepmother to Eliza Coonie and Hugh Coonie, 75; warrior activities and customs, 76

Daklugie, Asa: comments to Eve Ball about New Testament, 89; Geronimo's nephew, 63; greets Ove, 15; leaves Whitetail after wife's death, 64; as prisoner of war, 63; Robert Geronimo's father-in-law, 56

Dutch Reformed Church: Berle Kanseah describes former pastor [unnamed], 121; interpreter Solon Sombrero, 79; location at Whitetail, 88; missionaries at, xv, 137n 1; Sunday services at, 88

Enjady, Delores: close friends with Doris G. Ove, xvi; as cook at Whitetail school, 82; pregnancy of, 82–83

Geronimo: death of, 47–48, 74; on education, xxvii; keeps order in Mt. Vernon, Alabama prison camp classroom, 137n 1; and relationship with son Robert, 48, 49; resists U.S. military, x

Geronimo, Maude Daklugie, 54–55

Geronimo, Robert: birth of, 48–49; crafts a bow and arrow in traditional manner, 56–57; daughter Ouida meets Ove, 57; education of, 49; marries three wives, 50; meets Ove, 54–55; memories of father Geronimo, 51, 56; mother Ih-tedda, 48, 50–51; sitting on Ove's porch telling stories, xv, 55

Griffen, William B., 39

Griswold, Gillett, xx

Hardin, Lonnie, and family: driving skills of, 94; and marriage to Beulah, 141n 15; as principal at Mescalero school, 94; relieves Ove of teaching duties, 94; tells Ove to ignore violence, 100

Hostosewit, Levi: as bus driver, 60; Comanche heritage, 60; duties of, 61; meets Ove, 24, 61

Hugar, Elbys: describes conditions at Whitetail, xii; describes Dahteste (Old Lady Connie), 36–37

Istee, Charlie: anecdotes about Charlie and wife Dora, 67–68; concerned about future, 68; describes Warm Springs Apache warfare strategy, 65–66; driving a tractor, xv; as father of Evans, 68; recalled by Vernon Simmons, 105; sitting on Ove's steps telling stories, 16; as son of Warm Springs Apache Chief Victorio, 16

Istee, Evans: marital problems of, 68; murders his wife, 70

Johnson, Arthur: cooking meals with Ove at Whitetail school, 81; explains mother-in-law avoidance, 80; family problems, 81

Kanseah, Berle: on children and grandchildren, 124; and concerns about Apache language, 119; and connection between healing and language, 123; describes prayers at harvest time, 121; interviewed by Ove, 119–24; and opinion about preserving Chiricahua Apache history, 123; as Ove's brightest student, now member of Mescalero Apache Tribal Council, xv; remembers grandfather Jasper Kanseah, Sr., 122; on traditional religion and Christianity, 119

Kanseah, Jasper, Jr., 76

Kanseah, Jasper, Sr.: as a boy, 37, 75; disciplines granddaughter, 33; as grandfather, 75; marriages of, 75

Kanseah, Kathleen: ancestral relationship with Mildred I. Cleghorn, xxix, 47; de-

scribes what it means to be a Chiricahua Apache, 85, 133
Kanseah, Lynette Kazhe: interviewed by Ove, 122–24; as a mischevious child, 118
Kazhe, Dorcie: as a cook at Whitetail school and childern Peter and Lynette, xv; duties at Whitetail school, 117; friends with Doris G. Ove, xvi; interviewed by Ove, 113–19; death of father, 114–15; describes conditions at Mescalero Apache Reservation, 115–16; describes life at Phoenix Indian School, 113–14; meets future husband Isaac Kazhe, 114; relations with mother-in-law Emma Toklanni, 116–17, 142n 5

Landrie, Bill, and family: anecdote about relatives, 96; duties at Whitetail, 96; son Jimmy, 97

Mescalero Apache Reservation: accidents, deaths, disappearances, and violence at, 99–100; Ove's first visit to, 3–6; receives former Chiricahua Apache prisoners of war, 135n 3
Moorhead, Max, 40

Opler, Morris, 39
Ove, Doris Gils: close friends of, xvi; housekeeping skills of, 10–11; learns to drive, 14; marries Robert and moves to Whitetail, xvi, 6
Ove, Patricia: visit to Whitetail (1993), xviii
Ove, Robert S.: goes to Tribal Court, 100–101; impressions during 1992 visit to Whitetail, xxv–xxvii; interviews of, 105–24; and job at Whitetail, 3–6; leaves Whitetail, 125–26; life goals of, xvii; memories of, 127–28; pets of, 19–20, 121–22; photography as a hobby of, 17; questions Charley Smith's expertise as a medicine man, 140n 9; and recollections of Chee, Hugh, 70–75; and recollections of Chihuahua, Eugene, 58–60; and recollections of Coonie, Hugh, 76–78; and recollections of Daklugie, Asa, 63–64; and recollections of Enjady, Delores, 82–84; and recollections of Geronimo, Robert, 47–58; and recollections of Hostosewit, Levi, 60–63; and recollections of Istee, Charlie, 64–68; and recollections of Istee, Evans, 68–70; and recollections of Johnson, Arthur, 79–81; and recollections of Kanseah, Jasper, Jr., 76; and recollections of Kanseah, Jasper, Sr., 75–76; and recollections of Sombrero, Solon, 78–79; relieved of teaching duties, 94; responsibilities of, 24; shown how Apaches shave, 93; teaching technique, 30, 32

Phoenix Indian School, 113–14

Ruidoso residents: Cook, [first name not remembered], pharmacist, 97; McCoy, Miles, retail store manager, 97; Moore, Larry, M.D., 98–99; sheriff [full name not remembered], 97

St. Joseph's Catholic Mission, Mescalero: Bucher, Father Marcian, 90–91; Chiricahua Apaches' first exposure to Catholicism, 90
School at Whitetail: bus and drivers at, 23, 60, 79; Christmas pageant at, 34; classroom size of, 26; class trip to Ranger station, 28–29; delousing students at, 117; fire at, 62; Ove and Arthur Johnson as cooks at, 81; Ove's responsibilities at, 24; physician and dentist at, 25; protection against wild animals, 13; shower facilities at, 118; sign of, 23; site of community activities, 26–27
Simmons, Vernon: cooking outdoors, 106; describes Eugene Chihuahua's house, 110; describes locations of houses at Whitetail, 113; grandmother Hernannie, 141n 1; interviewed by Ove, 104–13; recites anecdotes about scout Kuni, 112;

Simmons, Vernon (*continued*)
and recollections of Chihuahua, Eugene, 106–109; and recollections of Dahteste (Old Lady Coonie), 106; and recollections of Istee, Charlie, 105; taboo about owls, 111
Skinner, Woodward, 137n 1
Smith, Charley, Jr.: as medicine man, 87; and origin of family's name, 87; Ove questions expertise of, 140n 9; and posing for a picture, xv
Sombrero, Solon: education of, 78; how his father was named, 78; interpreter for the Dutch Reformed Church, 79

TenHaken, Bernice: quotes Belle Kazhe regarding missionaries, 140n 12
TenHaken, Reuben: as church pastor, 88; Ove visits, 89; recalled by Berle Kanseah, 119

Thrapp, Dan L., 140n 10
Tissnolthos, Wheeler, 88
Tribal store, Mescalero: bulk supplies, 93; owner Juan Baldinado, 92–93

violence: at Ruidoso, 98; at Whitetail, 98–100

Whitetail: climate of, 17–18, 20–21; as described by Elbys Hugar, xii; Dutch Reformed missionaries build church at, xii; living conditions of (1913), xi, xvi; school at, 22–35; typical day for Chiricahua Apaches at, xiii; water problems at, 11–12; weekly social events at, xvii; wildlife and birds at, 13–14, 16–17
Worcester, Donald E., 141n 16